THE GREAT ESCAPE
Newport County 2016-17

THE GREAT ESCAPE

Newport County 2016-17

ANDREW PENMAN

St David's Press

Cardiff

Published in Wales by St. David's Press, an imprint of

Ashley Drake Publishing Ltd
PO Box 733
Cardiff
CF14 7ZY

www.st-davids-press.wales

ISBN
Paperback: 978-1-902719-68-9

British Library Cataloguing-in-Publication Data.
A CIP catalogue for this book is available from the British Library.

Typeset by Replika Press Pvt Ltd, India
Printed by Akcent Media, Czech Republic

CONTENTS

This book is dedicated to long-suffering Newport County fans everywhere and to my wonderful wife Claire for putting up with being a football widow.

PREFACE

I've been reporting on the fortunes of Newport County AFC since joining the *South Wales Argus* sports desk back in 2007.

It's been a decade of ups and downs for the club, but mostly ups with two unforgettable trips to Wembley and two priceless promotions.

I've watched hundreds of matches from the less than luxurious press boxes at Spytty Park and Rodney Parade and at countless stadiums across England – from Braintree to Blackpool and Lewes to Leeds United.

Over the years I've clocked up more miles than Jeremy Clarkson and visited Reading service station more times than I have some of my closest relatives.

Two matches stand out above all others during my time following the Exiles up and down the country.

The first is the 2013 Conference play-off final when the club finally completed its journey back to the big time after 25 years in the non-league wilderness thanks to goals from Christian Jolley and Aaron O'Connor.

And the second is the final match of the 2016-2017 season as Michael Flynn's men staved off the looming threat of relegation in the most dramatic circumstances imaginable in front of a packed Rodney Parade.

The journey that Flynn and his team went on in those final 12 matches was a joy to report on and it's been a pleasure to relive the whole extraordinary story of the most turbulent of seasons.

In writing this book I've attempted to take readers behind the scenes – onto the training ground, inside the dressing room and behind the manager's office door – to tell the full story of the Great Escape.

ACKNOWLEDGEMENTS

Thanks first of all to Mark O'Brien for scoring the goal that made this book possible and to my publisher Ashley Drake for giving me the opportunity to write it.

Thanks too to everyone at the *South Wales Argus* and Newport County AFC, especially Michael Flynn, Gavin Foxall and Hayley Ford for their help, and to Julian Davies at Davies Sports Photos for providing access to the club's photo library. Thanks also to the guys at *Eat Sleep Footy Repeat* for the use of their images of that historic day in May 2017.

FOREWORD

Professional football has been my life for almost 20 years now but the 2016-2017 season has to go down as the most incredible experience of my whole career.

I've always said I'll do anything to help Newport County AFC – my hometown team and a club I love - and I certainly took on a lot of roles in an extremely eventful 10 months. I started out as director of football and business development before I was brought back as a first team coach and then as a player by Graham Westley. I'll always be grateful to Graham for the faith he showed in me but after he left the club I didn't have to think for long when I was asked to take the job of caretaker manager. That's four roles for a start, and I'm sure there were a couple of others I was doing without realising as well, but you need that with small clubs like Newport – you need everybody chipping in and helping wherever they can. What we achieved in keeping this great club in the Football League was exactly that – a team effort.

I was the one in front of the press and the TV cameras as we worked our way to completing the Great Escape but I certainly couldn't have done it on my own. The board of directors were brilliant with me. They gave me the chance and they backed me all the way.

Wayne Hatswell, one of the best coaches in the division in my book, was the first man I called when I knew I was taking over for the final 12 matches and he proved to be worth his weight in gold. I always believed that we could avoid relegation and Hats kept telling me again and again that we would do it in the final game. With seven minutes to go against Notts County I nearly strangled him but he was right in the end, and what a way to do it!

The experience of Lennie Lawrence was also invaluable for a new manager like me and he was a fantastic calming influence during the tough times – like the thrashing we took at Plymouth.

The fans' support for me and the team was also a massive part in the successful run we had and I'll never forget celebrating with them on the pitch at Rodney Parade, and in the pubs of Newport after that dramatic finale, but the vast majority of the credit has to go the players who went out there on the pitch and produced the goods time and time again.

As you can imagine, they were all pretty low after being torn apart by Leyton Orient. As a coaching team we tried to put a smile back on their faces and take some of the pressure off them and they responded superbly, producing an amazing seven wins in 12 matches and earning 22 points from a possible 36. Two months after that humbling at home to Orient we completed the Great Escape in the most dramatic circumstances imaginable.

Mark O'Brien will go down in the history of the club as the man who scored the goal that secured our place in the Football League but every member of the squad played their part, from Joe Day in goal to Ryan Bird in attack. O'Brien, Mickey Demetriou, Scot Bennett, Dan Butler and David Pipe worked wonders in defence, with the help of Darren Jones, Sid Nelson and Jazzi Barnum-Bobb, and Demetriou turned into a regular goal machine at the other end of the pitch as well, earning us priceless wins against Crawley and Yeovil.

In midfield, Mark Randall produced his best football for us when it really mattered, as did Tom Owen-Evans who scored a vital first goal on an unforgettable day at Exeter. Captain Joss Labadie started the ball rolling with the winner at Crewe in my first game in charge and played a massive role, as did Sean Rigg and our loan star Alex Samuel.

Aaron Williams, Mitch Rose, Jaanai Gordon, Jennison Myrie-Williams and Marlon Jackson also played their part in what we achieved, as did those who didn't get onto the pitch in those unforgettable two months.

Lastly I have to thank my wonderful wife Victoria and all my family who helped me keep it together during a pretty stressful time.

My focus is now on the future and making sure that we don't find ourselves in the same situation again but the 2016-2017 season will stay with me forever, as I'm sure it will with everyone who was involved and all those who witnessed that final day drama at Rodney Parade.

I've known Andrew since I returned to Newport in 2012 and he's the perfect man to tell the inside story of the Great Escape. He was there with us every step of the way over those 12 games reporting for the *South Wales Argus* and this book is a brilliant way to remember what we all achieved.

Michael Flynn
Manager, Newport County
September, 2017

INTRODUCTION

In the early years of the 20th century, world famous escapologist Harry Houdini performed some of his most spectacular feats in what was then the town of Newport, when the Budapest-born showman kicked off his very first international tour at the town's Lyceum Theatre in 1905.

On his second visit he upset local police chiefs by escaping from a cell in Newport police station, naked and handcuffed. The *Weekly Argus* newspaper reported how an 'astonished' police chief witnessed a fully-clothed Houdini emerge from the cell after merely four minutes.

Houdini next returned to Newport in 1913 – the year after the formation of Newport County AFC – and, while performing at the Newport Empire, he announced his intention to leap into the River Usk from Newport Bridge.

After employing a lookalike to engage the attention of the police, a naked and handcuffed Houdini made his way to the opposite side of the bridge and lowered himself in. Upon miraculously freeing himself from his bonds and swimming ashore, he returned to the Empire that evening and, according to the *South Wales Argus*, was greeted by a 'magnificent reception' from his audience.

Six decades on from Houdini's stupendous stunts Newport County's footballers, led by manager Colin Addison, pulled off the club's first Great Escape. County won their last five matches – including a final day home victory over Workington – to avoid the prospect of being voted out of the Football League in 1977.

In May 2017, 40 years later, caretaker manager Michael Flynn and his players completed the greatest of Great Escapes. He may not have been naked and handcuffed but Flynn's achievement in guiding his hometown club to safety would surely have earned the respect of even the great Houdini.

To say County were in a tight spot when Flynn replaced Graham Westley in March 2017 is something of an understatement. The Exiles had just been blown away at home by fellow strugglers Leyton Orient, losing 4-0, and were hurtling towards relegation from the English Football League. The defeat left County 11 points adrift of safety with just 12 games left to play and a return to non-league football looked all but inevitable.

The last time the club had lost its Football League status, in 1988, it went to the wall within nine months. Reformed by a small group of supporters shortly afterwards, it took the new club 25 years to return to the elite group of 92 clubs.

Over the course of a quarter of a century there are so many people who made immense contributions that it is impossible to include a comprehensive list, but the likes of honorary president David Hando, chairmen Chris Blight and Les Scadding, directors Howard Greenhaf, Mike Everett and Matt Southall, volunteers like Lisa Savage and promotion-winning managers John Relish, Graham Rogers, Tim Harris, Dean Holdsworth and Justin Edinburgh all played a huge part.

A return to the big time was finally secured under the guidance of Edinburgh on an unforgettable day at Wembley in May 2013. Goals from Christian Jolley and Aaron O'Connor sealed a 2-0 win over Welsh rivals Wrexham in the Conference play-off final. Achieved with the backing of Euromillions lottery winner Scadding, the club then became fan-owned in 2015 when he moved on.

The Supporters' Trust took control as the fans raised more than £200,000 to complete the deal but, after just four seasons back in the Football League, the club was only going in one direction under unpopular boss Westley.

Flynn was handed a mammoth task when he was asked to take the reins after Westley was sacked in March 2017 but, in the words of World Cup winner Thierry Henry, he made the impossible possible.

Six wins in 10 games lifted the Exiles out of the bottom two after more than 200 days in the drop zone. Defeat in the penultimate match at Carlisle United, however, meant the spectre of relegation was still hanging over the team going into the season finale at home to Notts County.

Flynn's men knew they had to win to be absolutely certain of survival and, with relegation rivals Hartlepool United beating title-chasing Doncaster Rovers, County were heading for the drop with just seven minutes of the season remaining. The hopes and dreams of 7,000 fans inside Rodney Parade, and thousands more around the country and beyond these shores, rested on the 11 men playing their hearts out on the pitch.

It was the unlikely figure of defender Mark O'Brien who stepped up to the plate in the 89th minute to preserve the club's Football League status and become an instant Exiles hero.

This is the full story of a tumultuous campaign at Rodney Parade – from the optimism of the summer of 2016 under Warren Feeney, through the bleak midwinter of Westley's turbulent reign and the ultimate triumph of the Great Escape under hometown hero Flynn.

Supporters can relive the highs and the lows of what was an extraordinary 10 months, even by the standards of a club well used to turmoil and upheaval. All the key figures have their say and, with fresh insight from

Flynn, co-chairman Gavin Foxall and others, this book is a memento of a truly remarkable story.

"We're Newport County, we fight to the end," was the refrain of Flynn and the fans as the campaign reached its thrilling climax and everyone involved in the greatest of Great Escapes lived up to that mantra.

Andrew Penman
September, 2017

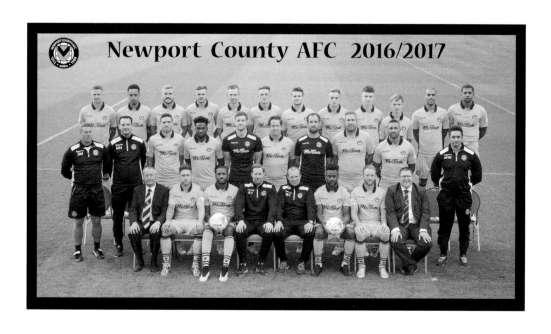

Newport County AFC 2016/2017

1

There Will Be Blood

"League Two is tough but I think we've got the players and the staff to get out of this league. You look at teams like Leicester winning the league – they've given everyone hope"
Newport County midfielder Mark Randall

The summer of 2016 was an unforgettable one for Welsh football as Chris Coleman's national team confounded all expectations by reaching the semi-finals of the European Championships in France.

It was followed, however, by an autumn of discontent for the nation's four major clubs with Newport County AFC, Swansea City, Cardiff City and Wrexham all stumbling out of the blocks as the new season got under way, and all four sacked their managers in a tumultuous 15-day period between the end of September and the middle of October.

Newport County were the first to blink. The board of directors decided to terminate Warren Feeney's contract as they travelled back from watching the 1-0 defeat at Grimsby Town on September 27. Coming as it did after a run of just one win in 22 matches, the decision did not come as a shock and was welcomed by the majority of the club's fans with a season-long battle against relegation in prospect.

RANDALL: COUNTY CAN PUSH FOR PROMOTION

A confident Mark Randall's prediction for the 2016-17 season

It was a far cry from Feeney's fine start in Newport in the 2015-2016 season. He arrived as John Sheridan's assistant in October 2015, leaving his role as manager of Linfield in his native Belfast to help Sheridan revive a club that was on its knees following Terry Butcher's brief spell in charge.

Sheridan inspired the team to a 10-game unbeaten run in all competitions to move County away from the relegation zone but, after losing three of his final four matches in charge, the former Republic of Ireland international was tempted by a move closer to his family and he jumped ship to League Two rivals Notts County in January 2016.

Feeney stepped up to the top job to replace Sheridan with the Exiles in 20th place in the League Two table – just three points above the relegation zone. Many supporters and pundits feared that the club's precarious position meant the job was too big to be entrusted to a rookie manager.

Feeney had enjoyed a successful playing career with the likes of AFC Bournemouth, Luton Town, Cardiff City and Swansea City and won 46 caps for his country but his coaching CV boasted only short stints as an assistant at non-league Salisbury City and at Newport, and a season in charge of Linfield in the semi-pro Northern Ireland Football League Premiership.

It was all smiles at the pre-season friendly against Weston-super-Mare

Former County player Michael Flynn was, however, adamant that the appointment was the right one. Flynn, who had been brought back into the club in a coaching role under Sheridan and continued under Feeney, told the *South Wales Argus* in January 2016: "You'll always get doom-mongers talking about experience but you've got to get the right people in who are hard-working, with the right contacts and who want to do things the right way.

... but Warren Feeney found himself under pressure as the new season began

"You've got to get experience from somewhere to be able to get experience. Let's be honest – we've tried experience in the past and it hasn't always worked out but Warren has been at Salisbury and Linfield. He's not got 10 years of experience as a manager but what he has got is experience of playing at the top level. He's been dealing with players at the top level and lower level players, dealing with managers, agents, chief executives – he's got all that experience.

"That's the kind of thing people don't see and just because you haven't got a CV of 10-years' experience it doesn't mean you're going to fail. I'm confident that we'll make this work."

Initially, together with new assistant manager Andy Todd, Feeney and Flynn did make it work as County won six of Feeney's first 11 matches in charge to move 13 points clear of the drop zone, but that form could not be sustained and a run of eight defeats and no wins in the final 11 games of the season saw the club finish 22nd in the table.

Feeney's men were nine points clear of relegated Dagenham & Redbridge in 23rd but such a dismal end to the campaign saw the manager lose any momentum that he had built up and lose the support of a fair proportion of the Rodney Parade faithful.

Despite murmurings of discontent from the fan-base there was never any prospect of him being moved on at that stage, according to co-chairman Gavin Foxall: "If you appoint a manager you've got to back that manager and as a board we were backing Warren," said Foxall. "He'd met the objective of keeping us up the season before and therefore we wanted to support him with his players that he wanted to bring in. There wasn't any thought at all about whether he was the right person to do the job. He needed the opportunity to build on keeping us up and that's what we asked him to do."

He may have had the support of the directors but there was no doubt that Feeney was under pressure as he prepared for the 2016-2017 campaign and that was only increased as the majority of the squad departed in May and June 2016. He released eight players as Yan Klukowski, Matt Partridge, Seth Nana-Twumasi, Rhys Taylor, Joe Green, Nathan Ralph, Scott Barrow and Dean Morgan were not offered new contracts and, while he offered new deals to Mark Byrne, Andrew Hughes, Darren Jones, Alex Rodman, Danny Holmes, Scott Boden, John-Christophe Ayina and Medy Elito, only veteran defender Jones opted to stick around.

It left Feeney with a major rebuilding job on his hands and, with one of the smallest budgets in the division, it was by no means easy to recruit a whole new squad that would be able to hit the ground running and be competitive. A total of 15 permanent signings and five loan players came through the door at Rodney Parade before the end of August. Amongst

Warren Feeney organising his team in the pre-season friendly with Forest Green Rovers

The Newport players take the field, to face Mansfield, for their first league game of the season

those signed up were former Arsenal midfielder Mark Randall, ex-Cardiff City striker Jon Parkin and youngsters Rhys Healey and Josh Sheehan on loan from Cardiff and Swansea respectively.

Off the field, Feeney brought former Premier League striker Sean McCarthy into his coaching team to replace Flynn, who was moved to a specially created role as football and business development director. Flynn managed to disguise any disappointment he felt about being sidelined as he discussed his new job and County's prospects for the season ahead: "It's an exciting and challenging job," he said at the time. "I have always been willing to help this club in any way I can; it's bigger than any one individual and is about the people who have been here through thick and thin.

"I want to try and bring in some new investment so that we can progress the club in the long term off the field as well as on it. It's a different role for me but I'm a people person who can sit, listen and get across the benefits of getting involved with the club. That's something I am excited about, it's not going to be easy but I am confident we can achieve it."

Looking back, after the season had ended, however, Flynn admitted that he was hurt by Feeney's decision: "I realised that he wanted his own man in," he said. "I had a couple of text messages from Warren when I was abroad and when I came back from holiday we had a meeting.

"I was disappointed because I knew I had something to offer and I didn't really see it coming, but that's football. He wanted his own man in and I understood that. I'm big enough to accept that and move on."

Discussing the new job created especially for him, Flynn added: "It was an interesting role and I put a lot of effort into it but did I enjoy it? Not really – you want to be out on the grass."

Despite his disappointment, Flynn maintained his support of Feeney as he previewed the campaign ahead in August 2016: "It was a disappointing end to last season and because of that people forget the good work Warren did," he said. "Nobody wants to go so many games without a win but in a way it could be a blessing in disguise. Players that Warren might have kept he has decided to let go because he wants more consistency.

"Warren has built a strong squad this summer – he's been able to bring in the players he wants to and the board have been very supportive and, as long as injuries and suspensions don't hit them too hard, I think County can definitely surprise a few people this season."

After a team-bonding pre-season trip to Poland, new signing Randall was confident enough to predict a promotion challenge before a ball had been kicked in a competitive fixture: "We've got a really good squad. I think the gaffer has brought in some really good players this summer," he said. "I don't want to jinx anything but I think if we do it right we'll do really well this season.

"I know sometimes it does take time to gel when there's a lot of new players but we're a close bunch, good friends, and I think whatever happens on the pitch we'll look after each other. League Two is tough but I think we've got the players and the staff to get out of this league. I don't see why not," he added. "You look at teams like Leicester winning the league – they've given everyone hope. We've got to believe in ourselves and each other to do it."

Speaking on the eve of the first match of the season at home to Mansfield Town, Feeney was more circumspect but he too cited Leicester City's extraordinary 2016 Premier League title triumph as an inspiration: "We're never going to be a team that's going to have the biggest budget in the league," said the manager, "but I look at Leicester. They don't [have the biggest budget] but if you get a good team spirit and you get the right players you will be competitive.

"We're looking at around the bottom six [in terms of budget] but I never use that as an excuse because Leicester for me is the benchmark. It was about staying up last season, no matter how we did it," he added. "We did it and there has been a big overhaul in the summer. I think it was needed and I think I've brought in better players than we had.

"I'm not going to say I can wave a magic wand. We're still a new group and we're still learning and gelling together but I think we've got players with the right mentality. They will take their time and get used to each other in the league but I'm confident that there's enough ability in that changing room that we'll be OK this season."

The Exiles' playing budget for 2016-2017 actually placed them 22nd out of the 24 teams in League Two, which was exactly where they were to finish nine months later.

"There's obviously a definite correlation between money and success on the field," conceded Foxall. "There are some clubs that break that mould – like Accrington Stanley – but there is a correlation. It was a case of giving Warren an opportunity to build a squad with his players over that summer and, with the players he brought in and the support that we gave him, I think we thought we would be a mid-table team."

2

A Bridge Too Far

"I found Warren to be a very decent bloke. He wanted to do his best for the club but it just didn't work out"
Newport County co-chairman Gavin Foxall

Warren Feeney fielded 10 summer signings on the opening day of the new season – August 6, 2016 – with goalkeeper Joe Day the only survivor from the previous campaign but there was no bright new dawn. Despite fighting back from 1-0 and 2-1 down, County ended up pointless

Jordan Green, left, and Sean Rigg, right, celebrate with goalscorer Jamie Turley at Leyton Orient

as Kevan Hurst hit a 93rd-minute winner for the visitors Mansfield Town and, although there'd been a marked improvement in terms of performance compared to April and May, it was a result that had the doom-mongers predicting another season of struggle at Rodney Parade.

Another stoppage-time goal led to another 3-2 defeat and an early exit from the EFL Cup at the hands of MK Dons three days later. It was now 13 games without a win and Feeney admitted that he was up against it, but he insisted that it was unfair to judge him on his record at the end of the previous season: "I think there is pressure," said the Exiles boss. "A lot of people talk about last season but my objective was to keep the squad up. I did that and it's a fresh start now. People will always talk and look at it and it [the 13-game run without a win] is a fact but I am starting afresh with my own team and I don't look at what happened last season. We did enough to get over the line and that's all I was asked to do.

"Fans will always talk about it," he added. "I don't do social media but I keep hearing it if I meet people in the street. Football is probably the hardest job in the world that everyone will have an opinion on but I came in after two managers and my objective was to keep them up. I did that and if I wanted to keep all those players I would have, but I didn't.

"It's a big turnaround with 16 players [coming in] and it's the second competitive game for the boys. There's only Darren Jones who signed on and Joe Day is still here but it's a new group of players and a fresh start – whether it was a new manager coming in at the start of the season or not.

"It was tough last year to get players out of a lull and I don't think Houdini would have changed it," he added. "You can see at the moment I think we do have the right mentality. That's all I focus on – that changing room – and I've seen enough to turn this around. I'm confident that these boys, as we get working together and playing together, can turn this around."

A 1-0 win at Leyton Orient on August 13, courtesy of defender Jamie

Warren Feeney knew the tide was turning against him as his side was beaten at home by Cambridge

Joss Labidie struggles to control the ball in the abandoned match against Barnet

The players were literally fighting to save Warren Feeney's job at Blundell Park

Turley's first-half strike, gave Feeney a brief respite but that was as good as it got for him and his team. Three successive draws – at home to Crewe Alexandra, away to Hartlepool United and at home to Cheltenham Town – left the Exiles with six points from six games, two points above the drop zone, and the abandoned home clash with Barnet on September 3 – due to a waterlogged pitch – was a sign of the problems that were to dog the Rodney Parade playing surface throughout the campaign.

The 2-0 loss at promotion favourites Doncaster Rovers was not disastrous but the 2-1 reverse at home to bottom club Cambridge United was. The team was booed off as they dropped into the bottom two following another late winner for a visiting team at Rodney Parade. Feeney faced calls for his head from the crowd and knew that he was clinging on to his job as he and the team made the long trip to Grimsby the following Tuesday.

On the night that Sam Allardyce was forced out of the England job after an elaborate newspaper sting, the County players certainly fought to save their manager from a more routine sacking.

They battled manfully at a gloomy Blundell Park and looked set to earn another point. Then, two minutes from the end, left-back Dan Butler pulled the shirt of Tom Balarinwa in the box and Omar Bogle scored from the spot to condemn County to a fifth defeat of the season.

It left the Exiles bottom of League Two and left Feeney sounding like a beaten man as he hit out at Butler after the final whistle: "I'm getting sick of it," he said. "It's not even a basic mistake – it's embarrassing, to be honest. I can't accept that and I said that to him. I can't accept what he's done. The players worked so hard. I thought it was a fantastic performance. They played for each other, they played for the club and to get done by that it is hard to take. You can't coach that. I'm lost for words on it. I can't get my head around what he's trying to do. It was a rush of blood to the head. I thought he played decent for 88 minutes and he goes and does that. It's unacceptable."

The board of directors made the decision to sack Feeney and assistant Andy Todd that night: "We played really well at Grimsby but then gave away a penalty right at the death and that was it," recalled chairman of the operations board Gavin Foxall. "I was the one that delivered the bad news to him. There was a number of us who went up to the game in two cars and we were then in a conversation on the way back to Newport. I then rang Warren that night when he was on the bus.

"He knew it was a difficult situation and a difficult decision for us, one that we didn't take lightly. We met him and Toddy on the Wednesday morning and then asked Sean McCarthy and James Bittner to take charge for a period of time. I then spoke to Scot Bennett to explain where we were and asked him to relay the message to the team."

The announcement was made the morning after the Grimsby defeat, with coach McCarthy and goalkeeping coach Bittner placed in charge of team affairs on a temporary basis. Captain Bennett spoke for the

The boss knew time was up for him after defeat at Grimsby

players after the news broke, with nearly all inside the dressing room genuinely sad to see Feeney and Todd go.

Bennett posted a message to fans on Twitter: "Absolutely gutted waking up to the news on the gaffer and Toddy being sacked. We as players have really [let] them down with costly mistakes. [He is a] top manager and a top bloke and all I can do is wish him the very best in the future."

Speaking before Feeney's departure, Bennett admitted the players had underperformed: "I think he's built a really good squad and we're trying to play for him," said the skipper at Grimsby's Blundell Park. "We're all really behind him and sometimes the fans have got to look at the players. It's us making the mistakes – not him. I know he's picking the team but we're the ones making the mistakes.

"We feel we should be further up the league," he added. "We should be up near the top with the squad we've got and it's really frustrating that we keep making these mistakes, but if you keep doing it then you can't keep saying it's hard luck. We're all trying to put in a performance and I feel we did today. The lads worked really hard and unfortunately it's just a silly mistake."

Bennett revealed that Butler had apologised to his teammates in the dressing room at Grimsby: "It's frustrating when we've played so well and then in the 88th minute we get the chance to put the ball in the stand and unfortunately Buts isn't quite thinking," he said. "He's had a really good game and then he's tried to play it off the player instead of just putting his foot through it and that's cost us.

"I think we're all feeling bad but when you're the one that makes that mistake [it's worse]. You go in and you have words because you've got to dig people out sometimes when things go against you but he came straight in and he apologised. He's down and we've just got to pick him up now."

Looking back on the start to the season, Foxall finds it hard to pinpoint exactly where it went wrong for Feeney: "It's difficult to put your finger on one thing but we're in a results business and obviously the table didn't lie," he said. "It was a unanimous decision, there wasn't really a debate about it.

"The first eight or nine games we were losing to late goals. It was difficult for Warren to take because it was a very close thing in terms of results but, understandably so, the fans looked at it as X amount of games without a win going back to the season before.

"Football is an opinion-based sport and everyone had a view on that but I've got a lot of respect for Warren. He's a decent bloke and he put everything into making it work. Sadly it just didn't work. We're in a results-driven game and we had to make a change accordingly. Those boys have been around football for a long time and they understood that it's not personal. I found Warren to be a very decent bloke with a lovely family. He wanted to do his best for the club but it just didn't work out for a number of reasons."

Foxall also insists that the pair parted on good terms: "It's always difficult when you lose your job but I think he'll do well," he said. "On the morning when we were announcing the new manager I rang him to tell

Caretaker managers Sean McCarthy, left, and James Bittner were in charge for just two matches after Warren Feeney was sacked

him out of courtesy. He texted me on my wedding day to wish me all the best and I sent him a message of congratulations when he got the job at Crawley [as assistant to former Liverpool star Harry Kewell]. These things are never personal and I do hope he does well."

County are a club for whom the expression 'it never rains but it pours' could have been coined and the home clash with Stevenage, scheduled for October 1, became their second match of the season to be postponed due to a waterlogged pitch. As a result, the McCarthy/Bittner management team was to last for only two games.

The EFL Trophy match at home to a Swansea City development team was watched by the two main candidates to replace Feeney on a permanent basis and it was significant that, while Mark Yates watched from the stands, Graham Westley was pictured chatting to the chairman of the owner's board, Malcolm Temple, in a hospitality box during the match.

3

Help!

"Whether people like Graham Westley or not I don't think he's bothered and the fans and the chairman won't mind if the team is doing well. If the team buys into how he likes things done then they will be successful"
Newport County striker Craig Reid

The directors called upon two Newport County AFC legends for advice as they looked for the man to secure the club's hard-earned Football League status.

John Relish, who played in the 1977 County team that pulled off the club's first Great Escape from relegation and later won promotion as the reformed club's first manager, was consulted, and so too was Michael Flynn, a key part of the team that had won promotion via the National League play-off final at Wembley in 2013.

Flynn played a big role in helping to decide who would land the job. The board wanted to put his football knowledge to good use and asked him to speak to the candidates and report back with his recommendations.

"We spoke to Graham Westley, Mark Yates and four others, so there were six in total," explained co-chairman Gavin Foxall. "We wanted to undertake the process in the right way and engage people in the right way.

"We had a conversation with John Relish, somebody who as a board we respect a great deal and the fans do as well and Flynny played a big part in the whole recruitment process as well, speaking to a number of candidates."

Flynn was happy to be involved after being marginalised under Feeney: "The decision on who got the job was nothing to do with me but the board asked me to help out," he explained. "I spoke to a few managers to see if they'd like interviews, I spoke to managers who had applied for the job and the board got a shortlist together. They did everything in the right way and I was just in there as experience for me – to see how the interview process goes – and for advice on football matters."

Former Exiles star Reid backs Westley for job

Graham Westley is tipped to take over

Foxall revealed how he and his fellow directors went about getting the right man for the job: "We decided as a board to have an approach whereby we'd identify certain candidates that we felt were right and could do the job," said the chairman of the operations board. "We also got applications in and we approached a number of people. Our long list was pretty long and then we got it down to a short list, which was a mixture of those that had applied and those that we'd contacted ourselves.

"Flynny was instrumental in all of that," he added. "Knowing football in the way that he does he undertook hours of conversations with different people to get advice and that got us down to six candidates.

Sean Rigg acknowledges the travelling support after the 0-0 draw at Colchester, with new manager Graham Westley watching from the stands

'1 BELIEVE IN OUR SQUAD'

New manager Westley insisted the Newport squad was strong enough to survive in League Two and there'd be no dash to sign new players in January

"We did two lots of interviews, speaking to them each once. Basically what we asked them was to outline what they would do in the first 90 days. All the candidates were strong candidates who understood all about us as a supporter-owned club. It's quite a therapeutic process to sit back and listen to somebody external give a view on the club about many different things."

The rescue team of Graham Westley, left, and assistant Dino Maamria

Speaking a few days before the final decision was made, former County striker Craig Reid told the *South Wales Argus* that Westley was the right man to get the club out of trouble at the bottom of League Two: "I have a huge amount of respect for Graham and I think he'd be the perfect person for Newport in the position they're in at the moment," said Reid, who previously played under Westley at Stevenage and was to team up with him again at Newport in January 2017. "The way he goes about things means you will get a hard-working, strong, disciplined side. He leaves no stone unturned in his preparation for the opposition.

"He knows that league, and the league above having got promoted with Stevenage, and his experience and knowledge of that level would be ideal."

Westley's unorthodox methods had not proved popular with players and fans at some clubs, notably Preston North End, but Reid was a big fan: "Everyone hears rumours about Graham but he gets results," he said. "Whether people like him or not I don't think he's bothered and the fans and the chairman won't mind if the team is doing well. If the team buys into how he likes things done then they will be successful."

When it became clear that Westley was a serious candidate to replace Warren Feeney at Rodney Parade there were questions raised about the way he had conducted himself at previous clubs, but stories of him texting players with team selections in the middle of the night and motivating others by asking them to imagine their mother had been kidnapped did not deter the County directors.

Malcolm Temple, chairman of the owners' board, insisted Westley was always the man that they wanted to replace Feeney: "Gavin and I spent a day exchanging emails about targets," he said. "We had four and I think this was the one we really wanted. We headhunted him. He wasn't an applicant. We went to him and it was quite apparent when we interviewed him that he was the outstanding candidate. He was head and shoulders above everyone else."

Foxall agreed that the decision was a unanimous one and said they knew what to expect: "Graham Westley was the outstanding candidate, without a shadow of a doubt," he recalled. "I don't think anybody on the board suggested that that wasn't the case and we appointed him accordingly.

"We kind of knew what we were going to get with him, to a certain extent. He's a strong-willed character, there's no doubt about that. We had some good robust conversations but that is reflective of the way I am and the way Graham is as well.

"He's not everyone's cup of tea and he brought his controversies with him but you look at some of the stories and you think 'so what if he's texting people at 2am? Turn your phone off!' I had texts from him at 2am. He was like a machine. He didn't stop. He just had an ability to drive, drive, drive. That is the man he is, he's a very driven individual but it's just how you react to things.

"The guy had the record in this environment and hindsight is a wonderful thing," he added. "I don't think there were many people who thought 'that is an awful appointment, what are you doing?' I don't think we could have foreseen what then happened."

Flynn added: "The decision was down to the board and it was the right decision. I think 90 per cent of people at that time said we'd got the right man."

Westley was duly appointed on Friday, October 7 – just nine days after Feeney had been dismissed. He watched from the stands at Colchester United the following day as the Exiles battled to a 0-0 draw to remain bottom of the table after 10 games.

Sitting alongside the former Stevenage, Preston North End and Peterborough United manager was his long-term number two Dino Maamria. The rescue team was in place and ready to get to work.

4

A New Hope

*"Whilst he might just have a favourable start, make no
mistake this guy falls out with everybody!"*
Anonymous letter to the South Wales Argus

Graham Westley was officially unveiled at the Wales National Velodrome in Newport on Monday, October 10, and his appointment was widely welcomed by the Exiles fans.

There were dire warnings from Preston North End and Peterborough United supporters about what to expect and an anonymous letter was sent to the South Wales Argus predicting that it would all end in tears.

"Whilst he might just have a favourable start, make no mistake this guy falls out with everybody!" the letter-writer warned. "The players will soon tire of his arrogance and pre-historic methods and if he doesn't finish up getting you relegated then I will be shocked to the core."

Yet his impressive record at Stevenage, where he led the team from the Conference to League One in successive seasons between 2009 and 2011, suggested he was just what Newport County AFC needed in their battle to beat the drop.

Somewhat ironically, given the way things turned out over the following months, one of the first things Westley said to the

The new manager endeared himself to the fans at Yeovil

Despite the 1-0 loss to Yeovil, the supporters believed Westley was the man they needed

media on his arrival in Newport was: "We need to come together. I hope that this group of people can come together, find a winning way and produce a formula that gives the fans what they want, which is a winning football team.

"I've seen a goalkeeper [Joe Day] who could be playing in the Championship very easily and I've seen a lad in Ben Tozer who looks like a Championship player all over and that's just to name two players. There's plenty of ingredients here. It's just a question of harnessing them, forging a way that they all believe in and buy into and forging a way that gets the very best out of the lads that are here at the football club."

Westley also laid out his ambition to climb the ladder again after being sacked by League One clubs Peterborough and Preston: "I don't want Preston to be the biggest job I ever have," he added. "I want to make sure that I get something bigger and do better with it than I did there.

"If I'm going to get that sort of opportunity the next job I do, which is now this job, has to be a sensational one. I have to grab hold of this football club and produce an incredible performance."

It didn't quite work out that way but, after defeats in his first two games at a rain-soaked Yeovil Town and at home to Plymouth Argyle when Joe Day was sent off, things did take a turn for the better. A 2-2 draw at home

Jazzi Barnum-Bobb, left, and Rhys Healey both scored to give Westley a first win at Accrington

to Barnet on October 25, courtesy of a coolly taken 89th-minute penalty by Sean Rigg, got Westley and his assistant Dino Maamria off the mark at Rodney Parade. It was the start of a seven-match unbeaten run that gave the County fans hope of a brighter future and soon had Westley hinting at a fanciful-looking challenge for the play-offs.

The Exiles ended October with a superb display at Accrington Stanley to earn a 3-1 win against the play-off contenders. Second-half strikes from loan stars Rhys Healey and Josh Sheehan, and fellow youngster Jazzi Barnum-Bobb saw County overpower their Lancashire hosts and earn only their second victory of the season. It was followed by a slightly fortuitous draw at minnows Alfreton Town in the FA Cup and a 2-0 EFL Trophy win over AFC Wimbledon in front of just 368 fans at Rodney Parade who saw the debuts of Jack Jebb and Josh O'Hanlon, who'd arrived outside the transfer window as free agents, becomming the first of 16 new arrivals during Westley's five months in charge.

Off the field, the new manager also made the shrewd move of bringing Michael Flynn out of the wilderness and back into the coaching set-up to replace the departed Sean McCarthy.

"He knows the football club and one of the most important things when you come from afar is to make sure that you've got someone really close who is bang on your side who is helping you understand the football club," explained Westley. "You have to make sure you don't make basic errors by not understanding the people that you're working with and the club you're working with. I think it's vital that you are prepared to integrate into the football club. Don't expect, as a manager, to get respect from people if you don't respect the football club – it's very much a two-way process."

Reflecting on his return to the coaching set-up, Flynn insisted he'll always be grateful to Westley for the faith he showed in him: "I was delighted," said Flynn. "I think Graham liked the way I conducted myself during the interviews and in the conversations we had and I haven't got anything bad to say about him. He worked hard when he was here and he tried to help the club that I'm very fond of. Graham and Dino made a good team and I learned a lot from them. I was doing my UEFA Pro License at the time and I just wanted to keep learning on the job."

On the field, the upward curve continued as further goals from Sheehan and Healey earned a deserved 2-0 home win in the league over previously unbeaten Carlisle United, before Alfreton were finally dispatched 4-1 after extra-time in the FA Cup first round replay whilst Saturday, November 19, looked like being a red letter day for the club as they thumped a lacklustre

Rhys Healey slots in the opening goal against Carlisle at Rodney Parade

Notts County side managed by former Newport boss John Sheridan to climb out of the bottom two.

Goals from Rigg and the irrepressible Healey and Sheehan either side of half-time silenced the Meadow Lane crowd as Westley's men crushed the Magpies 3-0 and ensured Exiles fans were looking up the table with excitement.

The players also gave the new manager's approach the thumbs up, with defender Darren Jones one of many to extol the virtues of a tougher training regime: "I think the board have made the right decision to bring someone in now," said Jones. "He's got a lot of time to change it and I'm sure we can make the points up this side of Christmas and then hopefully push up the table.

"I'm sure the results would have changed [under Warren Feeney] because I do think we've got the right players here but whether it was a bit of bad luck or we weren't working hard enough I don't know," said the centre-back. "The board made a decision to bring Graham in and I'm sure he's going to push us in the right direction. His attention to detail is spot on and with the work-rate we do every day I'm sure the lads will be a lot fitter.

There was more joy for the Exiles at Notts County

"We've gone from zero to a thousand within two weeks," he added. "It's so much more intense. We're doing a lot more, we're getting stronger doing gym sessions two or three times a week."

Forward Sean Rigg reiterated that Westley had made the team fitter than they had been under Feeney: "Training has been harder," agreed Rigg. "Obviously the new gaffer is trying to raise our energy levels and our fitness. It is definitely more demanding and you do need that. Obviously it's a shock to the system initially but I do think it will help. At least we will go into games knowing that we're going to be the fittest team in the league and I think that confidence goes a long way."

County's climb from 24th to 22nd led Westley to suggest that his side could even be capable of a push for the play-offs: "We want to make sure that we give ourselves the chance in the second half of the season to be aiming for something in the league," he said. "We don't want to see our league season fizzle out. We don't want to be working towards mid-table at the end of the season, we want something more to play for. We can look at sixth place and think two or three weeks down the line it's realistic that we can put ourselves in contention."

After 18 months of decline since the departure of promotion-winning manager Justin Edinburgh in early 2015, the future once again looked bright for County, but there were storm clouds on the horizon.

5

Casualties of War

"Graham Westley is an impossible man to work with. I've been in the game for 20 years and I very rarely fall out with anyone but he needs to learn some manners and start treating people with some respect."
Former Newport County club secretary Graham Bean

"We've improved performance, we know that," said Graham Westley after the 3-0 win at Notts County that had finally lifted his side off the bottom of League Two and out of the relegation zone for the first time since September. "Now we need to show our strength of character

Rhys Healey impressed but County slipped to a 1-0 home defeat against Wycombe

Darren Jones in action at Blackpool, where things began to unravel for County and Westley

by making sure that improved performance leads to more, that we don't rest on our laurels and start thinking that we've achieved something.

"We've taken an important step in leaving the bottom two behind and we now need to build on that and make sure that we keep progressing forwards. Football's a funny old thing; you can't forecast from one week to the next what's going to happen."

What happened next was an unfortunate 1-0 home defeat to Wycombe Wanderers as Sido Jombati's 88th-minute free-kick beat Joe Day and sent Newport County AFC straight back to the bottom of the table.

"Things were definitely moving in the right direction under Graham," recalled co-chairman Gavin Foxall. "But it was similar to when John Sheridan came in the year before in that a lot of the decent results were either draws or they were in the cup. We were grinding out results but they weren't wins. You could see the potential and you could see that the team was a lot fitter than it had been."

However, as was to become clear the following week, things really started to unravel for Westley with the trip to Blackpool on November 26. County recovered from a catastrophic error by goalkeeper Day, which led to the Seasiders opening the scoring after just four minutes, to level through prolific loan striker Rhys Healey, but Sean Rigg then saw his penalty saved and Blackpool ran riot in the final half hour to secure a comprehensive 4-1 win.

Days later it emerged that club secretary Graham Bean, who had only been at the club for around three weeks, was heading for the exit after falling out with the famously abrasive Westley. On December 1, County fans woke up to a report in the *Daily Star* alleging that Westley was 'under

Sean Rigg's penalty was saved as County were trounced 4-1 at Blackpool

investigation' by the club after a row over the team's accommodation on the trip to Blackpool.

The *Star* reported: 'Westley blew his top when he discovered rooms that had been booked for him and his squad at the team hotel in Preston were on the ground floor. He prefers to be on the top floor of hotels, but to make matters worse he was situated near an ice-making machine.'

The report continued: 'His outbursts led to an internal row that saw him blame club officials – despite the booking being made by a travel company. This led to allegations of bullying of staff, which the club are now investigating. It is understood that Wesley has already been warned about his attitude when communicating with people at the club."

The directors subsequently denied that there was any investigation into Westley's behaviour and claimed that they had "made the decision to part company" with Bean "in the best interests of the club."

Bean, however, insisted he had quit his post, telling the *South Wales Argus*: "Graham Westley is an impossible man to work with. I've been in the game for 20 years and I very rarely fall out with anyone but he needs to learn some manners and start treating people with some respect.

"I reported my concerns about him to the board and if he were to leave the club I'd consider returning but there's no way I'd be prepared to

Graham Westley was in an argumentative mood at Plymouth Argyle in the FA Cup

work with someone of his character. There are some good people behind the scenes at Newport County who work hard for the club and I wish them all the best for the future, but if they stick with Westley then I fear for them."

Barnsley-born Bean, a former policeman, had previously butted heads with Westley in his role as compliance officer with the Football Association a decade earlier.

"Graham Bean and Graham Westley had history and I certainly wasn't aware of that," said Foxall. "The bottom line is that the club secretary and the manager have got to get on. It's as simple as that. That's really important for a variety of reasons. That relationship is a really important one in the club and they have to be able to work together."

One of the Grahams had to go and, according to Westley, he forced the issue: 'I did resign in late November when I realised just how frustrating the job was to me,' he wrote in his *Football League Paper* column, 'but I was persuaded to stay when the club fired its secretary instead of letting me leave and I took on my sense of duty to give my heart to the job and fulfil my contract.'

Foxall remembers being shocked as he woke up to an email from the manager that had been sent in the early hours: "He did resign and it was a reflection of a man who very rarely sleeps, I think," said the co-chairman. "He sent an email at 4.35am, and I remember waking up to that email and thinking, 'What now? What has happened now?' People see us on a Saturday and people think it's all a bed of roses when they just see you sitting in the directors' box, but every day you'd wake up to something and at that time I was thinking, 'What on earth now?' What could possibly have gone on from nine hours before?"

A hastily arranged meeting at a local coffee shop placated Westley and he and his assistant Dino Maamria were persuaded to carry on: "I spoke to Graham and told him we didn't want him to resign," said Foxall. "We sat down in Caffe Nero at Spytty, which was a favourite of his and Dino's, and he relayed some of the difficulties that he had.

"I said to him 'we can see the improvements that you've brought and we really don't want you to go'. He then went off and took training as usual and carried on doing his normal thing and Graham Bean departed. To a certain extent it sorted itself out but it was just another episode of 'what the hell has gone on overnight?' You did start to think we shouldn't be sleeping! It was 24/7 and I just found it a little bit odd at the time."

Just days later, Westley was once again making the wrong type of headlines as he clashed with Plymouth Argyle manager Derek Adams following the 0-0 draw at Home Park in the FA Cup second round. The Exiles boss walked in on Adams' post-match press conference and attempted to listen in as his opposite number spoke to the media.

After being asked to leave by the Plymouth press officer, Westley eventually began to head for the exit, but not before Adams snapped, squeezing past Westley and through the interior door before slamming the exterior door behind him. With the Portakabin walls still shaking, Westley then clashed with a *Plymouth Herald* journalist who asked him to explain his actions.

"The press officer asked me to leave. So I left. That was it," said the increasingly irritated boss. "I was asked to come and have a chat with the press. I was asked to come and speak to the press so I walked into the press room, while the other manager was speaking. He is welcome to come and listen to me, I have got nothing to say that I am scared of him hearing. I stood on the side of the room politely. The press officer asked me to leave, I was a bit confused and bemused by it but I then left the room. He stormed out, his choice."

After being asked about the incident again by

Loan striker Rhys Healey returned to Cardiff City in January after Graham Westley upset Bluebirds boss Neil Warnock

the same journalist – *Plymouth Herald* football editor Chris Errington – Westley lost his patience.

"Shut up and listen to me," he said. "Let's move on pal, you're boring me now. Move on, you're being a clown."

Foxall believes the incident was overblown but he says it was another sign of Westley's refusal to conform to accepted football protocol: "I asked him what it was all about and his view was that it was a storm in a teacup," said the co-chairman. "The press love those things and I understand it but he is that way inclined. All managers are different. Would Warren Feeney or Flynny have done that? No. They're different to Graham. Does it make them better or worse? No.

"Graham wasn't somebody that felt the need to mix with the opposition after a game. Flynny and the coaching staff will have a drink with the other side after the battle. Warren did that as well but Graham never did and that was his choice."

Westley's unhappy knack of upsetting people surfaced again the following week when he got wind of what he believed was an attempt by Plymouth to unsettle in-form striker Rhys Healey, who was on loan from near neighbours Cardiff City. The manager persuaded 22-year-old Healey to talk to the media about the matter and that upset his parent club.

Bluebirds boss Neil Warnock said: "I disagree totally with what's happened and I'm very, very annoyed with Graham at the moment if I'm honest. To ask a young lad to face the media and talk about Plymouth I think is totally out of order and I'll be speaking to Rhys.

"I don't think he should have been placed in front of the media with the first question asking him whether he was going to Plymouth Argyle, he should be talking about Newport and it was totally unfair. The current situation is not helping. I believe you should talk manager to manager about things, not through the papers."

The sorry incident led to County losing the valuable services of Healey and ramped up the tension with Plymouth ahead of the side's FA Cup second round replay, a tie that took on extra significance for the winner, when the third round draw set up a mouth-watering trip to Anfield to take on Premier League giants Liverpool.

The replay was selected for live TV coverage by BT Sport and moved to December 21, with the winner set for a magnificent early Christmas present – a financial windfall that, for County at least, could have been the difference between survival and relegation back to the non-league wilderness.

6

They Were Expendable

"It is pretty clear that the players aren't doing enough. Nobody can say 'I have not been given a fair crack of the whip' or that they have not been given a fair chance."
Newport County manager Graham Westley

"I remember listening to the FA Cup third round draw," recalled Newport County AFC chairman of the operations board Gavin Foxall. "I was in my car in the car park at Asda in Caldicot and people must have thought I was a lunatic because I screamed 'yes!' at the top of my voice when we got Liverpool away."

In between the 0-0 draw at Plymouth Argyle and the replay on December 21 there were two further defeats in League Two. Graham Westley's men were beaten 2-0 at home by his previous employers Stevenage and then lost a bad-tempered game 3-1

County lost a bad-tempered game at Crawley when 13 players were booked

There was heartbreak in the FA Cup as County missed out on a dream trip to Liverpool after defeat to Plymouth

at Crawley Town when an incredible 13 different players were shown a yellow card.

That made it four successive defeats in the league and ensured the Exiles would be bottom of the pile at Christmas – four points adrift, albeit with a game in hand - and, with a potential money-spinning trip to Liverpool on the horizon, the club's focus was very much on the crucial FA Cup replay at home to Plymouth four days before Christmas.

"I knew we had to get past Plymouth but we'd gone down there and got a draw with 10 men and we knew that we were becoming a stronger team," said Foxall. "We were definitely up for it and the whole occasion was fantastic. There's not many positives in being involved in a football club because of the amount of time it takes that you don't spend with your family and what it costs and the crap that you take, but it's great to see the excitement around the city before a big game.

"It was a massive FA Cup tie, the cameras were there and we got more than 5,000 through the gates. The atmosphere was brilliant but it was just a shame the way it ended. The money would have been fantastic but there

Joy turned to despair against Portsmouth on Boxing Day

was also an expectation that we were going to do it and we were going to go to Liverpool and take thousands to Anfield. Those things can make or break a club, there's no doubt about it.

"Look at Cambridge playing Man Utd [in 2015] – they showed that if you use that money wisely it can really set you up. I thought we gave a good account of ourselves but it wasn't to be."

A crowd of 5,121 packed into Rodney Parade on a cold December evening as the bitter rivals played out another 0-0 draw. Thick fog made visibility increasingly difficult as the match progressed but fans inside the ground and those watching at home missed little and the drama only arrived in extra-time when Plymouth were awarded a penalty after County winger Jennison Myrie-Williams handled the ball in the box.

Paul Garita's spot-kick hit the post and Westley's team fought on, until defender Darren Jones chopped down David Goodwillie to concede a second penalty. Graham Carey made no mistake to finally break the Exiles' resistance in the 113th minute and send the Pilgrims on their way to Anfield.

It was a crushing anti-climax for the directors, the management team, the players and the supporters but, with the club's Football League status at stake, there was no time to dwell on that disappointment.

It all got too much for Spytty the Dog against Exeter on New Year's Eve

After a Christmas truce it was back to the League Two battlefield on Boxing Day and, despite County propping up the division, the majority of fans were still fully behind Westley. That was evident as goals from loan stars Josh Sheehan and Rhys Healey either side of half-time put the Exiles on course for victory against promotion hopefuls Portsmouth. At 2-0, supporters in the Hazell Stand behind the dugouts sang 'we've got Graham Westley' and the manager responded to cries of 'Westley, give us a dance' with a little jig on the touchline, but seconds later the mood changed as former Exiles favourite Danny Rose pulled a goal back for Pompey.

Kal Naismith then missed a penalty for the visitors but there was to be no let off as defender Enda Stevens levelled and midfielder Naismith made amends late on, hitting the winner from a free kick to condemn County to a thoroughly demoralising defeat.

Things didn't get any better on New Year's Eve as an Ollie Watkins hat-trick earned Exeter City a thumping 4-1 win at Rodney Parade and made it six successive losses for Westley's men. County still had a game in hand on the teams above them but they ended 2016 four points adrift at the bottom of League Two and five points from safety.

The manager, who said on arrival that he hoped he would not need to sign any new players in January, conceded that there needed to be a major overhaul of the squad once the transfer window reopened: "It is pretty clear that the players aren't doing enough," he said. "Nobody can say 'I have not been given a fair crack of the whip', or that they have not been given a fair chance. Everyone has had a chance. I have analysed and assessed what I have. We need people who can implement what we are telling them. I know exactly how many new players we need."

Westley was clear that the problem was not him. The problem was that the players he had at his disposal were not good enough: "I have won a lot of games as a manager, averaging a win every two games, but I haven't managed that here," he said. "Maybe I am not the problem, maybe there is a resource issue.

"There are a lot of promotions in our management team and collectively we believe we need better than we have got, in certain areas. It is important we have a good first week in

Graham Westley and coach Michael Flynn were putting together a long shopping list for the January sales

the window and make some changes and give ourselves the best chance of winning games on a consistent basis. Football is simple. When a team isn't functioning, always look at the spine," he added. "We are conceding too many, we aren't scoring enough."

One of Westley's many buzzwords during his time in Newport was 'ingredients' and he had a long shopping list: "We've got to do our very best to use our network, which is considerable as a management team, to see if we can attract people to the challenge that lies before us," said the manager. "It's not easy to be rooted where we are and it's a challenge to us all to show what we're made of.

"It's easy to feel sorry for yourselves and it's tough to find the answers but we're all here to find the answers and we're all working very hard. We're looking to find ways of making things happen and we'll keep working hard until we find the answers we need.

"We've now got the opportunity to do some work, to shift things around a bit and add some new ingredients. I do think the ingredients are needed and if we add the right ingredients I'm sure we can put a team together that can win football matches."

7

Back to the Future

"Sometimes a player comes along who's got a history of success with a football club. When you've got a player you know is going to be strong in the dressing room, who understands winning standards and demands them, it's a no-brainer to bring them back"
Newport County boss Graham Westley on the return of David Pipe

Graham Westley wasted no time in adding the first of his new ingredients as he signed two players within hours of the transfer window opening on January 1. Striker Aaron Williams arrived from Westley's previous club Peterborough United on an 18-month deal and fellow forward Jaanai Gordon was brought in on loan from Premier League West Ham United.

Williams played the full 90 minutes the following day at Wycombe Wanderers and a fortuitous goal from Mark Randall on the hour looked like halting the Exiles' losing run, but two strikes for the hosts in the final 20 minutes made it seven successive defeats in the league, which

Mark Randall gave County a shock lead at Wycombe but again it ended in defeat

Fans' favourite David Pipe was back in a County shirt at Stevenage

prompted more transfer activity at Rodney Parade.

First came two more loan moves, as young centre-back Sid Nelson joined from Championship club Millwall until the end of the season, and the following day veteran defender David Pipe returned to the club from non-league Eastleigh.

Pipe had captained County to promotion via the Conference play-off final at Wembley in 2013 and was a firm fan favourite but he had left the club under a cloud the following year after being deemed surplus to requirements by manager Justin Edinburgh.

Dan Butler found the net at Stevenage, where his performance caught the eye of co-chairman Gavin Foxall

"Sometimes a player comes along who's got a history with a football club," explained Westley. "A history of success. When you've got a player you know is going to be strong in the dressing room, who understands winning standards and demands them, it's a no-brainer to bring them back."

Returning to the club he loves was a dream come true for the former Wales international: "It's not only me coming back to where I live and where I've always lived, but the predicament the club is in and, without being big headed, I think I am what the club needs regarding the fight side of it," said Pipe. "Due to what happened in the past, I always wanted to come back to the club before my career was up, but I'm not here to wave goodbye, I'm here to fight.

"To come here and keep us in the Football League, where we need to be, would be a massive achievement," he added. "For me, it's 22 games and a massive amount of points to fight for, and we'll fight for every point."

Another former hero returned the following day as striker Craig Reid, who scored 66 goals in 112 appearances during his first spell for the club between 2008 and 2011, was signed on a free transfer from Gloucester City. Perhaps the most significant signing of the month and of the season as a whole, though, was made on the same day as a little-known Irish defender arrived on a free from League Two rivals Luton Town. Exiles fans did not know much about Mark O'Brien before he was brought in on January 6 but he was to have the biggest impact of all the new boys.

The new signings could not prevent an eighth straight defeat in League Two, however, as the misery continued at Stevenage on FA Cup third round day. As Plymouth Argyle were preparing to play Liverpool in front of the TV cameras and a capacity crowd at Anfield the following day, County were beaten 3-1 in front of just 2,185 fans at Broadhall Way.

Pipe, O'Brien, Nelson, Gordon and Reid all made their first appearances but Matt Godden's hat-trick sealed all three points for the hosts before a late consolation goal from defender Dan Butler.

Michael Flynn was delighted to be back on the pitch for his hometown club

Westley's insistence after the match that it had been "a very positive afternoon" did not go down well with fans, who were beginning to lose faith in the manager.

"It was always going to be difficult to start the game with five new lads in the side," he added. "That newness was always going to create a few misunderstandings here and there. It was inevitable that that was going to be the case but we showed character, strength and resilience to fight back and get our goal. So for me there were lots of positives."

The positives were not immediately obvious to anyone other than Westley that afternoon but co-chairman Gavin Foxall believes the match at Stevenage was important for one reason: "We saw the rebirth of Dan Butler there," he said, of the defender who would go on to be voted player of the year by readers of the *South Wales Argus*. "The boy had taken quite a lot of criticism but he came on when Jennison Myrie-Williams was injured, and for a lad who was only 21 to come back in that environment and score and play the way he did was amazing."

Westley was not finished in the transfer market and before the next match he added three more players to his squad. In came Kosovan striker Florent Bojaj on loan from Huddersfield United and unattached defender Mickey Demetriou, who was recovering from a series of injuries. Days later

January ended with what turned out to be a vital win over Hartlepool at Rodney Parade

striker Alex Samuel became Westley's ninth January signing as he made the short journey along the M4 from Premier League neighbours Swansea City on loan, but the biggest surprise of the month came when the team sheets were issued for the home match against Colchester United on January 14 when coach Michael Flynn was listed amongst the substitutes.

The 36-year-old midfielder had not played in the Football League since May 2015, making only a handful of appearances for Welsh League amateurs Undy Athletic in the meantime. Flynn's previous match for his hometown club had ended with him being sent off in first half stoppage time following a reckless tackle and alleged headbutt, something he now admits had a big bearing on his desire to pull on his boots again: "Ultimately it was Graham's decision," said Flynn. "I hadn't played in the Football League for 18 months but I'd played a couple of games for Undy.

"We had a lot of injuries in midfield and I've always looked after myself fitness-wise. I'm not as quick as I was and you'd never get 46 games out of me but I told Graham I could help us out in a sticky period. He said he'd have a look at me in the reserves and I played four games as centre-back and I really enjoyed it. He was impressed and I'll always thank him for giving me that opportunity to come back and coach and to give me a few more games.

"I didn't admit it at the time but a big part of it for me was because I didn't like the way my last one had finished in 2015," he added. "It was a

New signings Craig Reid, left, and Aaron Williams were jumping for joy against Hartlepool

tough period back then. I was coaching with the academy and juggling that with playing as well.

"I didn't really agree with what [caretaker manager] Jimmy Dack was doing with the first team. He was getting advised by Wayne [Hatswell] and sometimes listening but, a lot of the time, not. I felt hard done by a little bit and there was a lot of frustration there. I didn't mean to get sent off, obviously, and I still don't think I even touched him, but the referee deemed it as dangerous play and I got sent off in front of my little boy who was nine days old and watching his first game of football, and my last game. I didn't want to end my career like that so for me those four games I played in January and February were crucial."

Flynn was an unused substitute as County stopped the rot with a 1-1 home draw against Colchester and earned another point after a 0-0 stalemate at Barnet the following week, but he came off the bench in the 3-1 victory over Hartlepool United on January 28, a match that also featured signings number 11 and 12 of the month – midfielder Mitchell Rose and striker Ryan Bird.

Bird, Williams and a rejuvenated Butler scored to earn Westley's team a first win since November 19 as they closed the gap at the bottom of the table to just three points. It was a positive end to a month of wheeling and dealing from the manager and Foxall says the directors had felt a duty to give Westley every chance to turn the club's fortunes around: "You can't back a manager half-heartedly," he said. "If you're not going to back him you need to be honest and you make a decision, or they make a decision.

"We dug deep to see what we could do but it wasn't anywhere near what people thought it was in budgetary terms. The players that we picked up at that time were either at clubs that didn't want them or they'd been let go. Graham was able to attract those players at that time and some of them were pretty good.

"For a variety of reasons they just didn't gel under Graham but the fact that we retained a lot of them shows that they had something about them."

8

Apocalypse Now

*"You have to say they've not improved, they've got worse.
I want them to stay up but I just can't see them getting
out of it"*
former Newport County manager Warren Feeney

February began with a classic relegation 'six-pointer' at Cheltenham Town on a pitch that was almost as bad as the much-maligned Rodney Parade playing surface.

The County fans really enjoyed Jaanai Gordon's last-gasp leveller at Cheltenham Town

The Exiles led 2-0 at Cambridge before it all went wrong

Newport County started the match six points behind their hosts but a win would have closed that gap to three with a game in hand. Instead, they looked to be heading for defeat before substitute Jaanai Gordon slotted in a 93rd-minute equalizer to keep the unbeaten run going. It was unquestionably the highlight of the 21-year-old's loan spell and it was an unforgettable one for the 841 travelling fans behind the goal, who celebrated wildly with their heroes as another point was secured.

A creditable 0-0 draw at home to runaway leaders Doncaster Rovers followed – in a match that saw the only appearance of French free agent Maxime Blanchard, the 16th and final signing of Westley's reign, but there was very little romance in the air on a grim Valentine's Day evening as just 1,868 fans – the lowest league attendance of the season at Rodney Parade – turned up to watch another goalless game against Grimsby Town.

That made it six unbeaten for Westley's men and the manager was in positive mood after the match: "We're nicking a point here and nicking a point there and grinding away and that's progress," he said. "And all the time that we're winning a point here and winning a point there and staying unbeaten and getting a win we're pushing forward. I'd have taken eight points from six games and an undefeated record six games ago. This is a new team and we're only going to get better but it's a very solid start from the players."

Westley, however, had fallen out with key men Mark Randall and Ben Tozer and told them to stay away from training and co-chairman Gavin Foxall was less impressed with the run of 'positive' results: "We went on an unbeaten run again but they were draws rather than wins and it wasn't enough," he said, and the trip to Cambridge United four days later turned out to be the beginning of the end for Westley.

The day started superbly for the Exiles at the Abbey Stadium as a brace of sharply taken goals from Ryan Bird either side of half-time put them 2-0 up and on course for a much-needed victory, but what followed was an all too familiar collapse as the hosts fought back to 2-2 and then won all three points in controversial circumstances.

County midfielder Mitch Rose conceded a stoppage-time penalty and petulantly knocked the red card out of the referee's hand as he was sent off, earning himself a five-game ban in the process. Mark Roberts scored from the spot to end the unbeaten run.

Westley's men dropped two more points from a winning position as they were held to a 1-1 home draw by struggling Morecambe three days later, and the pattern was repeated at Mansfield Town as Bird gave County an early lead but the hosts fought back to take the points after another red card, this time for Gordon.

The red card for Jaanai Gordon proved disastrous for County at Mansfield

Just as he had at Cambridge, Westley again blamed a dubious sending off – with some justification: "It's a difficult result to take," he said. "We have to talk about a huge turning point in the where a sending off happens. We were confident and feeling good about the way we were playing at the stage and the sending off was a massive turning point – there was scarcely any contact."

The tide of public opinion was, by now, turning against the manager and he was confronted by angry supporters as he trudged off the pitch at Field Mill after a match that was also notable for the end of Michael Flynn's brief return to the playing squad, when he was forced off with a hamstring injury.

"Three games in a week didn't do my body any good," he said. "I had a few niggles due to age and not playing and unfortunately it was just tiredness where I pulled my hamstring at Mansfield. Dino and Graham did say 'sorry, we've over-used you and ideally we would have liked to have saved you' but it was just one of those things."

He didn't know it at the time but the next phase of his career was just about to begin and, looking back, Flynn is happy now to hang up his boots for good. Probably.

"That's it now," he said. "I can honestly look back on my playing career and be very proud. I hope I made my aunty, my mum, my uncle, my dad and my kids proud and, most of all, I can look myself in the mirror and say I gave my all and had a good career. If the worst case scenario happened and we had five midfielders injured and the transfer window was closed then you never say never but I can honestly retire happy now."

Westley was far from happy as his side entered the final two months of the season six points from safety and rooted to the bottom of the Football League. Managers generally don't like the label 'must-win game' but there was absolutely no doubt that the home clash with relegation rivals Leyton Orient fell into that category.

County started the day three points behind 23rd-placed Orient with a game in hand, and a victory would have seen them draw level with their opponents. The match fell on Westley's 49th birthday and attracted an increased crowd of 3,378 as the club offered tickets for just £10 but the party fell disastrously flat for the Exiles boss.

His side looked off the pace from the start and was simply ripped apart by an Orient team stuffed with teenagers and rookies. Steven Alzate opened the scoring in his first start before fellow 18-year-old Josh Koroma helped himself to a hat-trick – his first goals in professional football. County were beaten 4-0 and utterly humiliated. The players left the pitch to loud boos,

There was no way through for loan star Alex Samuel against Leyton Orient

while Westley could not have failed to hear the demands for him to resign or be sacked.

After speaking to the team, the manager gathered his thoughts as he looked out over the pitch from the lounge above the dressing rooms at Rodney Parade. Westley then engaged Flynn in a long conversation while reporters waited below for his verdict.

"Graham is an intelligent man and he always tries to analyse things," recalled Flynn. "When we went up those stairs I was thinking 'oh God! This is going to be a bad conversation'. Let's be honest, we didn't see any positives from that performance. We didn't see that coming and we spoke about that. We talked it through but then it was all about the next game."

When he did eventually speak to the media, Westley offered no defence of the performance but was careful once again to distance himself from any blame: "I'd be angry if I was the supporters," he said. "They pay good money to watch a team win and they want to feel that their team has given everything it can in the name of victory, and obviously the manager is there to take the flak in a situation where you can't get wins.

"I can justify myself, not that I need to, in terms of having inherited a team and a squad that was losing. I inherited a team that was right at the bottom of the league and to date I've not been able to turn that around. I've not been able to turn a losing situation into a winning situation. I am the person who has got to take the responsibility and take the flak. All I can do is come to work again next week and look for that little something and try to find it. I've found it often enough in my managerial career to date and I know that the job of work is not to start thinking in a negative way but to think in a positive way."

Westley trudges off after defeat to Orient

When asked if he was still the man to motivate the players, Westley said: "I think that these moments are moments where strong people stand up and are counted. I don't think they are moments where strong people show weakness or frailty. I think leadership is about making sure that when everybody else is in a grey and cloudy mood you are the sun in the sky, so to speak. It's up to you to help people to find a route forward, not to join the crowd.

"I'm not in the crowd, I'm in the managerial role – probably because I've shown leadership over the course of time. I've won a lot of games because I know how to win games and leadership is about being very, very strong when others doubt you but also being intelligent enough to look at situations and find different ways of doing things because if what you're doing isn't working then you have to alter the course."

With Hartlepool United, Accrington Stanley and Crewe Alexandra all winning, the devastating home defeat left County 11 points from safety and made it very difficult for anyone to be optimistic about their hopes of avoiding relegation. Westley's predecessor Warren Feeney certainly believed that County were destined for a return to non-league football, and Feeney was highly critical of Westley in an interview with the *South Wales Argus* published on the Monday after that Leyton Orient defeat.

"I look at the results and you have to say they've not improved, they've got worse," said the Northern Irishman. "I believe I would have turned

DON'T BLAME ME – FEENEY

Ex-manager Warren Feeney let his views on Newport's woes be known

things around. There were teams worse than us and it wasn't as if we were getting beaten by three or four – we were competing with teams. I was disappointed [to lose my job] and I think it was down to a little bit of a lack of experience on the football side on the board.

"The new manager," he added, "is now saying that the squad wasn't good enough but when he was appointed he was saying 'I've got good players' and they were good enough. He's got people like Ben Tozer with all his experience – who he said was a Championship player – and Mark Randall, who is a Champions League player, on the sidelines. He let Jon Parkin go and he's scoring goals for York and he said they'd be challenging for the play-offs by Christmas.

"Sooner or later you've got to stop talking and you've got to produce the results on the pitch. He's won one game in 20 and he's got no excuses. He's got his own players in and it's going to take a massive turnaround for them to stay up now. I had a great time there and met some good people and I know how hard the players work so I want them to stay up but I just can't see them getting out of it."

9

The Third Man

"There was nobody else we considered. I rang him at about 10.30pm and I think he would have come and met me there and then! He was raring to go"
Newport County co-chairman Gavin Foxall on appointing Michael Flynn

Graham Westley may have been determined to fight on but the Newport County directors had other ideas, and reports emerged on the Monday after that thumping defeat that the manager's position was in doubt.

"The Leyton Orient game started us having conversations," said chairman of the operations board Gavin Foxall. Were the players playing for him? I think the players looked tired. What frustrated me was that it was one of our first promotional games. Tickets were just £10 and the folk of Newport came out to support that and then that happened. It took me back to the game against Crawley the season before when we lost 3-0 and made the decision to part company with Terry Butcher. It was so disappointing.

"I wasn't in the directors' box that day," he added. "I was in my own box and I just sat there and thought 'God almighty, this is not good. Look

County 0 Leyton Orient 4

I'd be angry if I was a fan, admits Exiles boss Westley

The exit was fast approaching for Westley after this humiliating defeat

where we are'. You looked at the players on the field and started to think 'why is it they're not doing what they're capable of?'"

Deeply concerned by what he'd witnessed, Foxall decided to act: "I felt it was important that I spoke to some of the players, which I did, and they all relayed the same thing to me," he revealed. "They were tired, they were being worked too hard. That was their view and things weren't right. It was something that the board needed to address."

The BBC reported that Westley had been given two games to save his job but that was denied the following day by the County board.

"We had a conference call to discuss what we were going to do and we already had a meeting scheduled for later that week," explained Foxall. "At that meeting we decided to change things. We felt at that time, and I think many supporters felt the same way, that we were only going in one direction and that wasn't getting out of it. Therefore it was important that we made the change for the good of the club."

Westley's departure was announced on the morning of March 9 and this time there was to be no interview process. His successor was already in place and Michael Flynn needed no persuading to take the job, according to Foxall: "There was nobody else we considered," said the co-chairman. "I rang him on the night to tell him we were going to part company with Graham the next morning and we wanted him to step up. It was about 10.30pm and I think he would have come and met me there and then! I definitely didn't have to convince him. I told him to take the night to think about it but he was raring to go. Wayne Hatswell came up early the next day and they were both gagging to get at it."

Westley's response to his sacking surprised many supporters. Writing in his weekly column in

Interesting...

7:58 AM - 12 Mar 2017

Westley's response be being sacked became a talking point for many

the *Football League Paper*, he claimed he was glad to be out of Newport: 'I feel relieved to have left the Newport challenge behind,' he said. 'I wasn't having fun. I was not enjoying the slog. Everything was harder than it can possibly be if you are going to win consistently. It was a very difficult job over time to compete in the Football League with Newport's resources and the way those resources are structured.'

Westley listed the problems facing County as he saw them, including: the lack of a ground of their own; the 'difficult and demoralising' training surface; the poor pitch; the lack of administrative and support staff; the lack of an analyst, fitness coach, full-time physio and dedicated coaches and 'poor player recruitment.'

The former Stevenage, Preston North End and Peterborough United boss continued: 'I inherited a side that had won once in 24 games and, despite my best efforts, I only managed to win six of my 29 games. I moved a four per cent win rate up to a 20 per cent win rate. Even that was really hard graft. In leaving I can hold my head high though. I know I did good work. I believe the club invested in a League One manager to create a miracle, lost faith after the loss to Orient that it would happen and cannot afford my salary if they do slip into the National League. So they are taking steps before money issues get away from them. Simple. Understandable. I get that. It is fan owned and there is no big backer. Money matters.'

Looking back on Westley's time at the club, Foxall is full of respect for the efforts that the manager put into trying to save the Exiles from oblivion: "In terms of the standards of the club, he improved things immensely," said Foxall. "He was driven, there's no doubt about that. We knew that there were going to be challenges and at times he was a difficult chap to deal with. I didn't agree with everything that he did and we had some robust conversations at times, but I personally had a lot of respect for him in terms of the drive and determination that he had."

Flynn, also, has nothing bad to say about the man who brought him back into the coaching team and the playing squad and groomed him to be the next manager of his hometown club: "It would be easy to say it was all doom and gloom at that time but I didn't notice a lot of it if it was like that," insisted Flynn. "What the players spoke about between themselves I don't know. There was the odd bit of moaning and groaning here and there but all footballers moan, I've seen it a lot. I'm definitely not going to hammer Graham. One thing I didn't have to worry about when I took over was the players' fitness. He certainly made sure they were fit."

Were the players over-worked, as they claimed? "Maybe it was worse than we thought," he added, with a smile. "I best be a bit careful if the

FLYNN TAKES EXILES REINS

The fourth management team of the season is unveiled

chairman is speaking to the players. I'll make sure I give them their days off when they deserve it!"

Flynn has nothing but praise for the way he was treated by Westley and his number two Dino Maamria: "From the minute Graham brought me in he told me he wanted to make me ready to be the next Newport County manager," he said. "For me it happened a lot quicker than I expected, or wanted. I'm loyal and I gave my all with John Sheridan, Warren Feeney and the same with Graham, but I had a lot more say with Graham and my opinion was valued more and that was something I really appreciated.

"At first I had to get used to how Graham and Dino worked and I had to raise my standards. You'd forget something small and straightaway they'd tell you, and that's what you need. You don't need people just telling you you're doing well every day when you're not – that's how you learn. It was brilliant for me and it was a great learning curve."

With 12 games to save the club he loves and an 11-point deficit to claw back, the learning curve was about to get a whole lot steeper for Flynn.

10

Mission Impossible

"It is not impossible, it is going to be hard, it is going to be tough but we will keep fighting until the end as that is what the fans of this club deserve. Nothing is impossible"
Newport County manager Michael Flynn

Michael Flynn's career at Newport County was almost over before it began. As a teenager from the Pill area of the city he was a promising player but he was thrown out of the youth set-up for breaking club rules. Devastated by the decision, Flynn feared he would be stacking shelves in supermarkets or working as a postman for the rest of his life.

"We had two managers in the youth team at the time," said Flynn. "Glyn Jones had originally said that we weren't to play for any local sides, but we had a match called off and Roger Skyrme came in and said go and have a game. So I did."

Flynn duly scored a hat-trick for Pill in the Gwent League that

Michael Flynn, left, with County co-chairman Gavin Foxall

Saturday and the report in the *South Wales Argus* did not go unnoticed by Jones.

"It wasn't like the set-up is now with the education in place and scholarships, but it was my team, my club and when I was told to leave I was in bits," he said. "But I had the call from [Newport's then manager] Tim Harris to go and train with the first-team and that was that. I guess it changed my life but I was never going to give in and accept I wasn't going to make it. I'm not a quitter."

Flynn may not be a quitter but even he must have had his doubts that his beloved club could survive when he was unveiled as caretaker manager on March 10. Gavin Foxall, chairman of the operations board, admits that he and his fellow directors feared the worst: "I don't think we really believed we could get out of it," he said. "I don't think there was an expectation. I spoke to Michael and we agreed that the boys had had a lot of pressure on them because of the situation we were in. His job was to go in and be a bit more relaxed about things.

"We just wanted them to put a bit of pride back into the shirt and try to give the fans something to smile about after what had gone on. Because at that time the team was hurting, we were hurting and the fans were hurting.

"We never talked about whether we could survive, but Flynny - because of the kind of guy he is - was adamant that we would get out of it. He

Victory on road gives County fans new hope

By Andrew Penman
01633 777239
ape@southwalesargus.co.uk
Twitter @argusoncounty

Crewe Alexandra ... 1 County ... 2

Flynn soon saw his team picking up valuable points

kept saying 'we will get out of it, you know' and I just told him to take one game at a time.

"Of course I was thinking 'wouldn't it be brilliant if we did' but I didn't want him putting too much pressure on himself and thinking of it as a failure if it didn't happen. That was the danger because for him as a hometown hero it was a massive risk – what if he'd lost all 12 matches?"

Flynn tried to sound bullish when he spoke to the media ahead of his first game in charge at Crewe Alexandra. The new Exiles boss insisted: "It is not impossible, it is going to be hard, it is going to be tough, I am not going to dress it up as something it isn't, but we will keep fighting. We will keep going until the end as that is what the fans of this club deserve. Nothing is impossible."

He was well aware, though, of the risk he was taking in his first managerial role, as was his wife Victoria. He recalled: "When I got the call from Gavin I spoke to my wife and her first reaction was 'oh, bloody hell Michael!' I'm her biggest concern and she was saying to me 'do you want your first job to end with relegation?' But I knew we just needed to win a few football matches to get a bit of pride back.

"I thought we could do it. Was I confident that we could do it? Maybe not but I definitely wasn't writing us off. I knew if we got a couple of wins it could be done and, if we could do it, it was going to be huge.

"Of course it was a big risk," he added. "If I was the one to take the club down it would have killed me. It would have really upset me and bothered me for a long time."

Foxall was in no doubt, however, that Flynn was the perfect man to lift the players after the Leyton Orient humbling: "What he had was a knowledge of the players and what they were capable of," said the co-chairman. "He felt he could put his arm around the players and lift them and galvanise them and that's what he did.

Michael Flynn celebrates victory at Morecambe

Ryan Bird blasts home the winning penalty at Morecambe

"I went down to the training ground with Flynny and we spoke to the players. I said 'look, I know everything is quite difficult at the moment but we want to take a bit of the pressure off you and all we're asking as a board is for you to put a bit of pride and passion back into the shirt'. They delivered that in spades."

Pride and passion comes easy for Flynn where County are concerned and he worked hard to get the players similarly committed to the cause.

"The players definitely know what the club means to me," he said. "They could feel my passion and they could see how much I wanted to win, and they knew that I believed in them. I told them it was going to be tough but we had to give it a go and that we'd take it game by game."

First up was the trip to Crewe on March 11 and it looked like being the same old story for County as they fell behind midway through the first half and, with the hosts dominant, there was no sign of any great revival but, eight minutes after the restart, Dan Butler volleyed in to level the score and the Exiles' confidence grew as they began to attack Crewe with a renewed vigour.

They knew that draws would not be good enough in their predicament and they pressed hard for a winner, which duly arrived in the 88th minute as new captain Joss Labadie slotted in the winner to spark wild celebrations amongst the 200 travelling County fans in the Whitby Morrison Ice Cream Vans Stand at Gresty Road.

The win gave the supporters hope and increased the belief amongst the players that they could survive. The gap to safety was down to nine points with a game in hand – still a desperate situation but a whole lot better than it had been at the start of the week.

"Everyone in the dressing room believes that we can get out of this situation that we're in and that's exactly what we're going to do," said Labadie. "That is the first

The inspirational David Pipe shows his delight

time this season we've come from behind to win a game so we've shown great character and that's what it's going to need between now and the end of the season. We believe. We wouldn't be here otherwise. We're not done yet."

There was no time to dwell on the victory as the team was on the road again at Morecambe three days later. The players presented each of the 48 travelling fans with a County shirt to thank them for their commitment and they then rewarded them further with another vital victory.

A tight and tense encounter was settled by Ryan Bird's coolly taken penalty midway through the second half and Flynn's men held on through seven agonising minutes of time added on to claim another three points. It lifted the Exiles off the bottom of the League Two table and moved them to within seven points of Cheltenham in 22nd.

Match-winner Bird was in confident mood afterwards and full of praise for the impact of the new boss: "We don't look at points, we just take it each game as it comes and if we keep winning every game in front of us then we'll be flying," Bird said. "The last two performances have been fantastic and we can beat anyone in this league if we perform like that.

The players are congratulated by the fans at Morecambe

"When I came here that was my goal, to help Newport stay in the league. We had the belief anyway but the gaffer's given us the confidence to go out and play, express ourselves and enjoy it."

The morning after the Morecambe match Flynn received a congratulatory text from Arsenal and France legend Thierry Henry, a fellow student on the UEFA Pro License course run by the Football Association of Wales at Newport's Dragon Park and, looking back, he believes the psychological impact of winning two games back-to-back at the start of his reign was huge.

"Those first two wins were crucial," said the boss. "Going from 11 points behind to seven points in two games was huge. "And then with 10 games to go a seven-point gap looks a lot better than 11. You're down to single figures and you can start to claw it back."

11

Three Kings

"It's a good team. I really think we've got the best coaching set-up in the division. That's how highly I think of Lennie and Wayne"
Michael Flynn on Lennie Lawrence and Wayne Hatswell

According to Gavin Foxall, Michael Flynn's main impact on the players was psychological: "What Flynny did was come in and use his man-management skills to lift the squad," said the co-chairman. "I've been down to the training ground and the atmosphere is completely different to

Jaanai Gordon, left, and David Pipe take the fight to Blackpool

what it was previously [under Graham Westley]. Everybody has different methods and different thoughts on how you do things and that group of players reacted to him very well."

Foxall believes the difference in the players' attitudes was evident from the second half at Crewe in his very first match in charge.

"I've got a close relationship with him. He's a great lad and I was delighted when we won at Crewe," he added. "That second half was a completely different side. All of a sudden we were moving in a different direction, and then to go to Morecambe and win as well, it started giving people hope."

That hope was evident as Flynn received a hero's welcome when he emerged from the dressing room at Rodney Parade for the first time as caretaker boss and marched along the touchline in front of the Hazell Stand. The area behind the dugouts contains the most raucous and vociferous County fans and they are not afraid to make their feelings towards the manager known.

Just a fortnight earlier those same supporters were screaming for Graham Westley's head and all but the most optimistic left the ground convinced that their team was doomed to relegation. Two weeks and two wins later and the mood was transformed on the terraces and there was 100 per cent support for the new manager.

Unlike Londoner Westley, Flynn is Newport born-and-bred. The club means everything to him and the fans love him because of that, and that feeling was not dented by defeat to play-off chasing Blackpool in his first home game in charge on March 18.

The visitors silenced the fervour by taking an early lead and doubled their advantage with a dubious looking penalty midway through the second half. Promising youngster Alex Samuel, on loan from Premier League Swansea City, pulled a goal back and the Exiles pushed hard for a point, but Blackpool sealed the win with a third goal on the break in the fifth minute of time added on.

Frustrations boiled over at the final whistle and visiting manager Gary Bowyer claimed to have been hit in the mouth by a sweet thrown from the crowd. It was an unfortunate end to Flynn's first home match but Foxall had more serious matters on his mind during and after the game.

Alex Samuel gives County hope against Blackpool

"The Blackpool game could easily have been a draw," he remembers. "But in all honesty I wasn't that interested in the game because I was trying to help a guy who had a heart attack in the stand. Thankfully he recovered and came back in the stands a few weeks later but at the time, when a penalty was given against us and people were shouting and screaming all around us, we thought we were watching a bloke die in front of us. It put everything into perspective. It wasn't a nice afternoon but thankfully the Rodney Parade staff and the paramedics managed to save his life."

County were still in intensive care but they took another step on the road to recovery with a hard-earned point at home to Luton Town, another promotion-chasing team, on the following Tuesday. It was the second in a run of six games against teams who would go on to finish in the top seven and, once again, Flynn's men were behind before the fans' pre-match pies and pints were properly digested.

Young defender Sid Nelson, on loan from Millwall, made a rash challenge in the penalty area and Danny Hylton fired the Hatters ahead from the spot after just five minutes. A fabulous free-kick from Sean Rigg levelled the match in the first half but County's search for a winner was hampered when centre-back Mark O'Brien was sent off after picking up a second yellow card nine minutes from time.

The match was the Exiles' game in hand over their relegation rivals and, although a draw was not the result they wanted, it meant they closed the gap further on the teams above them in the table. They were now six points from safety but with only eight games left to play time was not on their side.

Rigg remained confident, however, predicting that the pressure would start to tell on their relegation rivals: "It's doable and the teams above us are under more pressure than us really because we've been written off," said the forward. "We're going into games with no pressure. We just want to enjoy ourselves. Teams like Cheltenham and Hartlepool have got more to lose than us and they're going to panic. One team always does seem to slip up at the end so we'll just keep going into every game playing with freedom and enjoying it and hopefully pick up the three points."

Scot Bennett shows his frustration as the game slips away at home to Blackpool

Rigg also backed the decision to replace Westley with Flynn, admitting that the players were feeling the effects of over-training: "Every manager is different," he added. "At the start of the season under Warren Feeney we didn't have a great start. When Graham came in he completely changed it. He put some fitness into our legs, which he thought we needed, and I think it helped to start with. But after a while I think maybe the boys tired a bit mentally and physically and I think maybe it was time for a change.

"Any club eases off towards the end of the season. You've got your fitness in and the games in so training doesn't need to be so intense, and I think that's going to help us a lot over the next eight games. We need to really look after ourselves and make sure we're ready to go in every single game."

Before the daunting trip to Portsmouth it was announced that former Cardiff City, Charlton Athletic and Middlesbrough manager Lennie Lawrence was to join the coaching team. The 69-year-old, who has more than 1,000 matches under his belt as a manager, was named first team management consultant.

The Exiles celebrate Sean Rigg's equaliser against Luton

Lawrence knew Flynn in his role as co-director of the Football Association of Wales' UEFA Pro License course. The master had been offering his pupil help and advice for weeks and Flynn was delighted to have such a wealth of experience on hand in an official capacity. He also expressed his confidence that his assistant Wayne Hatswell and Lawrence are better than any other coaching team in League Two.

"Wayne does most of the coaching," Flynn explained. "We have a meeting every morning and we talk through what we want to do and how we're going to do it. And we challenge each other. If I think what he wants to do isn't right I'll tell him why and we speak about it. Likewise, if he's not sure about something I want to do he'll tell me, and that's what you need. I don't want a yes-man.

"Lennie will chip in then and throw another spanner in the works and that gives us something else to think about. It's a good team. I really think we've got the best coaching set-up in the division. That's how highly I think of Lennie and Wayne."

Lawrence was on the bench with Flynn and Hatswell at Portsmouth on Saturday, March 24, as County looked to get the Great Escape back on track.

Alex Samuel scored again but it wasn't enough to avoid defeat

Marlon Jackson almost earned County a point at Fratton Park

Fratton Park had been a happy hunting ground for the Exiles since their return to the Football League in 2013. Flynn himself had scored both goals in a 2-0 win at the biggest stadium in League Two in December of that year and County had won there again in 2014 and 2016 – without conceding a goal on either occasion, but their luck ran out on their fourth visit to the famous old ground as Samuel was denied a penalty in the first half before the hosts established a 2-0 lead.

The Swansea youngster pulled a goal back 13 minutes from the end and substitute Marlon Jackson went close on a number of occasions but Pompey held on to claim the victory.

"We are in a difficult situation, but we are still fighting," said Flynn afterwards and, crucially, the teams above them in the table failed to take advantage of County's defeat. With seven games to go they remained six points from safety but Cheltenham and Hartlepool could not breathe easy yet.

12

The Longest Day

"We were stuck on the coach for two and a half hours longer than we should have been and we thought the game was going to get called off. It wasn't ideal preparation. But we never looked like losing that game"
Newport County manager Michael Flynn on an eventful trip to Exeter

pril Fool's Day saw the emergence of defender Mickey Demetriou as a goal machine when his spectacular long-range winner was enough to claim a vital victory over Crawley Town. Demetriou made light of the pock-marked mud-covered Rodney Parade surface as he skipped past a half-hearted challenge and unleashed an unstoppable left-foot rocket from 25 yards.

The win moved County to within five points of safety as Hartlepool United were beaten 2-0 at home by promotion-chasing Portsmouth. Cheltenham Town leapfrogged Hartlepool and maintained their six-point advantage over the Exiles as they won 3-1 at home to Morecambe, but there was a sting in the tail for Michael Flynn's men with captain Joss Labadie somehow managing to

Tom Owen-Evans @TomOwenEvans · Apr 8
Can't believe we haven't moved for over an hour 😩 Hope the fans are having a better journey @NewportCounty

County's transport woes as reported by Tom Owen-Evans

get himself sent off after an off-the-ball confrontation with Crawley's Welsh defender Josh Yorwerth, who also saw red.

It meant the skipper would miss the next three games through suspension and was a headache that Flynn could have done without at such a crucial stage of the season, but the manager was pleased with the effort from his players and, in particular, the dogged defensive display as they held on for the three points with 10 men.

"We've got 10 points from 18 now and it's been a big turnaround," said Flynn after the match. "I'm very pleased with the reaction from the players and the effort they've put in. They've got to keep doing that in every game. We've got six to go – six cup finals.

"I told the players I'm proud of them," he added. "They've given everything since I've been here and that determination, that effort and that intensity has got to last every game now until the end of the season. Nothing less than that will do.

Tom Owen-Evans takes aim at the Exeter goal

Tom Owen-Evans celebrates his goal at Exeter

"We've got six games to go and if we close the gap by one point every week we're going to stay up – that's what I'm praying for, but we've got to go and try to win every game."

The Exiles boss was delighted with the clean sheet but admitted his side needed to add more cutting edge at the other end of the pitch: "I would have much rather they'd finished some chances and it would have made it a lot easier on the side of the pitch when six minutes [of stoppage time] went up," he said. "It was heart in mouth time and if we hadn't won I would have been devastated. We've got to kill teams off when we create the chances."

Meanwhile, match-winner Demetriou insisted that the team was on course to avoid relegation: "The gap is five points and the most important thing now is that we're within two wins," he said. We could've been two or three up but we've shown how to win ugly at the end of it. We need

Michael Flynn congratulates match-winner Tom Owen-Evans at St James Park

to carry on doing that in the next six games. We're trying to get on a little run now and close that gap. The gaffer always goes on about making sure, game by game, if we close that gap then it's a good result."

Next up was what, in theory, should have been a simple trip across the Severn and down the M5 to Devon to take on play-off contenders Exeter City at St James Park. At just under 100 miles it was one of the shortest journeys of the season for County but the trip did not go to plan. An accident caused gridlock on the motorway and the match was almost postponed with the Exiles team bus stranded.

Eventually a police convoy escorted the players through the mayhem and the team arrived at the ground shortly before the scheduled 3pm kick-off. Both Cheltenham and Hartlepool were already ahead as the players completed their warm-ups in the Spring sunshine before the match finally kicked off 45 minutes late.

"We were stuck on the coach for two and a half hours longer than we should have been and we thought the game was going to get called off," recalled Flynn. "Hartlepool were winning and Cheltenham were 2-0 up at one point so everything was going wrong. It wasn't ideal preparation, but we never looked like losing that game."

After a tight and tense first half, the match was settled in County's favour on 53 minutes thanks to Tom Owen-Evans' superb solo effort. The 20-year-old academy graduate was picked out by stand-in skipper David Pipe and, finding himself in space 30 yards from goal, Owen-Evans ran at the back-pedalling Exeter defence before curling a left-foot shot into the bottom corner.

It was a first goal in senior football for the youngster after his earlier effort in the abandoned home game against Morecambe had been scrubbed from the record books but, more importantly, it earned a shock three points and was the perfect end to what had been shaping up to be a frustrating day for the team.

"Exeter were a very good side – they got to the play-off final," said Flynn. "It just shows you what a massive result that was and how good the boys could be. Mark Randall was outstanding that day on a nice pitch. His quality on the ball was incredible but he worked his socks off when he didn't have the ball.

"I was really happy for him after that game. It was nice to see a smile on his face. He's quite a quiet man and he's not big-headed at all so to see him so happy was great. I was delighted for Tom as well. After his goal against Morecambe had been ruled out he must have been wondering when he was going to score his first goal. What a time to do it. It was an unbelievable strike. When he hit I was thinking 'what is he doing here?' but he caught it sweet and it won us the game."

With Cheltenham and Hartlepool both letting their leads slip to draw, at Wycombe and Morecambe respectively, it meant Flynn's men had cut the gap to safety to just three points.

With five games still to play, the momentum was building and the mood in the County dressing room was buoyant. That was evident as the 1979 disco hit *Ain't No Stopping Us Now* blasted out of the team's inner sanctum

The County fans enjoyed their trip to Devon

Newport County AFC v Yeovil Town

County edge closer to safety with a third successive win

A 1-0 win against Yeovil and County's third successive victory

after the match. The McFadden and Whitehead song, widely interpreted to be about the experience of the African American community, has been adopted by various sports teams over the years, including the Philadelphia Eagles, the Detroit Red Wings and the Los Angeles Rams, and it perfectly captured the mood of infectious optimism and belief emanating from the County squad after that crucial win in Exeter.

"I don't think that was intentional," said Flynn. "I don't think I even noticed it after that game but I definitely noticed it after the next home game. It was great to see the belief growing and fair play to them for backing

Ain't No Stopping Us Now - the fans sensed the Great Escape was on

themselves because it takes a lot of guts and determination to do what they did."

It was a fourth win in seven games under Flynn, compared with four in 24 under previous boss Graham Westley and the optimism of the players was matched by that of the fans as 3,789 – the highest home attendance in the league up to that point – turned up to cheer on the team against Yeovil Town on Good Friday.

The queues for tickets spilled out of the main gates at Rodney Parade, down Grafton Road and onto Corporation Road. It was clear evidence of the growing belief that the Great Escape was really possible and hundreds were still waiting outside as the match kicked off. Some didn't make it to their seats before the midway point of the first half but they missed very little in a cagey opening to the match.

County gradually asserted themselves and edged ahead through a spectacular Demetriou free-kick just before the hour mark. The defender curled the ball around the Yeovil wall and inside the left-hand post from 25 yards to break the deadlock.

The fans sang 'The Port are staying up' and, despite missing several chances to extend their lead, a third successive clean sheet sealed a third successive 1-0 win, and with Cheltenham and Hartlepool both, once again, drawing, the Exiles were just one point behind Pools with four games left to play.

"We were in a good position then," said Flynn. "We were fighting hard and we'd matched the number of wins we'd had all season before that."

Ain't No Stoppin' Us Now was again blasting out of the County dressing room after the match. "It's superstition now," admitted Demetriou. "The last few games we've won we've had that on straight after the game. Obviously we need results to go our way as well but we know we can do it."

The Great Escape dream was gathering real momentum.

13

The Good, the Bad and the Ugly

"I was trying to talk to the team after the match and I was getting emotional. I could feel tears coming because I knew what it meant. We were so close to getting over that line"
Michael Flynn on defeat at Carlisle

Nine days after that shock win in Exeter and just three days after the home victory over Yeovil, Michael Flynn and his Newport County

A bad day at the office against Plymouth

squad headed back to Devon to renew acquaintances with Plymouth Argyle on Easter Monday.

The Pilgrims had already beaten Warren Feeney's County in the Football League Trophy in August, won at Rodney Parade in League Two in the early days of Graham Westley's tenure and Derek Adams' team had also knocked Westley's Exiles out of the FA Cup in December, thus denying them a dream trip to Anfield to take on Premier League giants Liverpool.

In their fifth and final meeting of the season Plymouth needed just a point to seal promotion to League One in front of a sell-out crowd of just under 14,000 fans. However, a run of five wins in eight games meant Flynn's men were confident of spoiling the party at Home Park and, with relegation rivals Hartlepool United taking on basement boys Leyton Orient at the same time, they knew it was vital to at least avoid defeat against Plymouth.

For the first 40 minutes of the match that looked a real possibility but one goal for the hosts five minutes before the break quickly led to a second and, as Plymouth turned on the style, the County defence was exposed time and again. The back line – minus the injured Mark O'Brien – that had kept three successive clean sheets was blown away by the men in green.

Plymouth ended up with six but it could have been 10 on a nightmare afternoon for County that threatened to inflict a potentially fatal blow

Sean Rigg shows his delight as he celebrates with goalscorer Mark Randall against Accrington

to their hopes of survival. A stoppage-time strike from substitute Aaron Williams preserved the record of scoring at least one goal in each game under Flynn but it was hardly a consolation for the 337 fans who had made the 140-mile journey.

Rookie boss Flynn admits the performance left him shell-shocked and he was grateful for the experienced head of Lennie Lawrence in the immediate aftermath: "After the game I wasn't sure what I was going to do or say," he remembered. "I wasn't sure whether to have a go at them or to try to butter them up, but Lennie stepped in. He said 'don't worry, I'll speak to them first.' I was a bit calmer after that but I was in shock because I hadn't see that coming. Plymouth are a very good but we didn't look like conceding six goals in any game, and it could have been eight, nine or ten on the day.

"Lennie went in and just told the boys that we couldn't change it now. It was a terrible result and a poor performance but we had to move on because the next one was the biggest game of the season. I had a few words then and so did Wayne [Hatswell] and we got on the coach and tried to put it behind us."

The relief is clear at the final whistle against Accrington

What certainly helped ease the pain was the news that free-falling Leyton Orient had rallied from a goal down to beat Hartlepool 2-1 at Brisbane Road. County's goal difference had taken a big hit, as had their confidence, but they remained just a point behind Dave Jones' Pools side with three games to play.

Alex Samuel is congratulated by County fans after another victory at Rodney Parade

"That was a big boost," said Flynn. "If we'd got a draw at Plymouth and they'd beaten Orient we would have been worse off so we were actually in a better position than we thought we would be."

Time for County to turn dream into a reality

By Andrew Penman
01633 777073
ape@southwalesargus.co.uk
Twitter @argu;oncounty @arguss-port

County .... 1 Accrington 0

Another home win

The caretaker manager did not panic after the Plymouth drubbing, letting the players take a break while he and his coaching team prepared for the visit of in-form Accrington Stanley: "We'd always planned to give them the Tuesday and Wednesday off and I know managers in the past who would have cancelled those days off and brought them in," said Flynn. "But we wouldn't have got anything out of the boys if we'd done that. We kept the two days off and when they came in on the Thursday morning we spoke for about 30 seconds on the Plymouth game. Then it was forgotten about and we got ready for Accrington. We knew that was a really tough game because they were 15 unbeaten."

Stanley came to Rodney Parade as the form team in the division and, after a big setback, they provided the sternest test yet of Flynn's motivational powers. Another crowd of 3,700 showed that the fans still believed that the Great Escape was on and the team repaid their faith with a superb performance.

David Pipe and Mark O'Brien recovered from injury problems to bolster the defence, while captain Joss Labadie returned from suspension in midfield and Ryan Bird was recalled up front. The striker scored the only goal of

Alex Samuel's injury at Carlisle was a big blow for County

the game on the hour, bundling in Mark Randall's effort on the line after great work from Alex Samuel to create the chance, but goalkeeper Joe Day was man of the match, saving his side time and again before and after the break and calming the nerves during another prolonged period of injury time at the end.

The final whistle was greeted with huge cheers and there was a party atmosphere at Rodney Parade as it was confirmed that Hartlepool had lost at home to Barnet. The Exiles had been in the League Two relegation zone for a grand total of 207 days but they were finally out of the bottom two. Having been 12 points behind Pools on March 4 and 11 points from safety, Flynn's team were now two points clear of the drop zone with two games left to play and they knew that finally their fate was in their own hands.

"That was arguably the biggest result because it got us out of the bottom two," said Flynn. "And when we got out it was down to us. It was a different situation then but I knew the boys would handle that pressure and they were superb. Game by game you could see their belief growing. Hats and I kept drumming it into them that we could do it."

Mickey Demetriou, left, and Mark O'Brien, right, couldn't contain the threat of Carlisle's Jabo Ibehre

County knew that they could even seal survival with a game to spare if they could win away against play-off contenders Carlisle United on the penultimate weekend of the season.

The squad travelled up to Cumbria on the train on the Friday and chairman of the operations board Gavin Foxall says there was a genuine belief that safety could be secured at Brunton Park: "Flynny and I went for a walk to discuss a few things the night before the Carlisle match and we both felt we could get the job done up there," said the co-chairman. "We were 32 minutes from doing it and, although we didn't deserve anything out of the match, you do start to think 'this could be our day'."

Mickey Demetriou's 12th-minute header – his third goal in six games – put County ahead against the run of play. At that stage, with Hartlepool losing to Cheltenham, the Exiles were on course to cement their Football League status. They led at the break but the tide turned when star men Alex Samuel and Mark Randell were forced off with injuries. Joe Day made a string of superb saves in the second half but the hosts' superiority finally told and they netted twice in three minutes to secure a deserved victory.

Flynn says the defeat affected him more than any other in his 12 matches in charge that season: "I felt more pressure and I got more emotional at the Carlisle game because I knew if we won up there that was it," he recalled. "So I was maybe a little bit more upset that we'd lost having been in such a good position at half-time. We deserved to lose it but that hit me the

Great Escape must be made the hard way

By Andrew Penman
01633 777239
ape@southwalesargus.co.uk
Twitter @argusoncounty

Carlisle Utd .... 2 County 1

The Great Escape would have to wait until the final game

hardest – even worse than the 6-1 at Plymouth. That's when it got to me a little bit.

"I was trying to talk to the team after the match and I was getting emotional. I could feel tears coming because I knew what it meant. We were so close to getting over that line but if we'd done it up there it would have denied us the Hollywood ending, and Hats said to me, 'gaffer, this is written in the stars. I'm telling you – we're going to do it at home.' He kept saying it and fair play to him."

Cheltenham's 1-0 win over Hartlepool meant that they were safe and it was a straight battle between County and Pools to decide who would survive and who would join Leyton Orient in being relegated. Flynn's men remained in the driving seat – two points clear of Hartlepool with one match of the season remaining. They knew that a win over Notts County at Rodney Parade on the final day would be enough to stay in League Two.

Carlisle manager Keith Curle spoke for everyone in the division when he declared his admiration for the job Flynn, Wayne Hatswell and Lennie Lawrence had done up to that point: "I think the manager and his coaching staff have done an absolutely phenomenal job," said the former England international. "Everybody in the second division thought Newport were down but credit to the staff and the players, they've got six wins out of 11 games, and they've got a home game now to take care of business."

After the match Flynn said: "It's a two-horse race now and only one of us is going to stay up. I said a few weeks ago we've got six cup finals and we're down to one now. I want to make sure we win so we're not checking our phones or listening to the crowd on how Hartlepool are doing. We've got to go and get the three points."

14

High Noon

"At times it sent shivers down my spine to think if we had gone down how would we then have recovered from that to come back up?"
chairman of the operations board Gavin Foxall

After 45 matches and more than 4,000 minutes of action, Newport County and Hartlepool United were separated by just two points.

Hartlepool had sacked manager Dave Jones on April 24 after an extraordinary intervention from celebrity fan Jeff Stelling live on his Sky TV show Gillette Soccer Saturday. "It's not personal Dave, but for God's sake for the good of the club go now," the presenter demanded after the 2-0 home defeat to Barnet. If he won't walk then sack him ... do it now, do it today."

Jones was duly shown the door on the Monday after Stelling's TV rant but caretaker boss Matthew Bates could not inspire his side to victory over Cheltenham Town in their penultimate game. A 1-0 defeat meant Pools simply had to

The big day arrives

beat already-promoted Doncaster Rovers at home on the final day to have any chance of overhauling County, and the Exiles knew that if Hartlepool did manage a shock win over the title-chasers then anything less than victory for them at home to Notts County would mean they would be relegated.

Flynn's men were undoubtedly in the box seat – a remarkable feat in itself considering their perilous position when Graham Westley was sacked in early March but, though they were on the brink of safety, it was still on a knife edge with the prospect of a return to non-league football all too real.

Gavin Foxall recalled: "In the week building up to the game Flynny would ring me up and say 'are you nervous?' and I would say 'well, I wasn't until you called!' But it was a nervy time, without a doubt."

Foxall admits that the board of directors had drawn up plans for relegation in the event that the worst happened: "Like any business, you need to make sure that you're planning for every eventuality and we certainly did that," he said. We would have lost at least £400,000. That was the Premier League part of the money, the rest of it was in a parachute payment, but

Michael Flynn tried to keep his players as relaxed as possible before the game

there were lots of different things that would have happened if we had gone down and it does not bear thinking about.

"I look at Hartlepool now and York, a great club with lovely people up there who are down in the division below the Conference. At times it sent shivers down my spine to think if we had gone down how would we then have recovered from that to come back up?"

Foxall was so concerned about the consequences of the results going against County that he would not take his family to the final match in case things turned nasty: "One of the sad things about the position we're in is that you do get some abuse," he said. "I've never minded constructive views but when it gets to personal abuse I don't think that's right.

"I'd said to my family that I didn't want them to come over and my eldest daughter had said she was worried about things. I told her the abuse goes with the territory but I told them I didn't want them to be there, and when we were heading for relegation I was glad they weren't there. It was an absolute nightmare."

The Foxall family may not have been inside Rodney Parade but an incredible 7,326 fans did snap up tickets for the eagerly anticipated season

Rodney Parade was packed for the finale of the Great Escape

finale. It was almost double the club's previous highest home attendance in League Two for the season and amounted to the biggest football crowd in Newport for 34 years.

Not since Easter Monday 1983, when 16,052 packed into the club's old Somerton Park ground for a local derby against Cardiff City, had so many attended a County home match. It was conclusive backing from the whole city for Flynn and his players and the club was delighted with the fans' response.

"As a collective we spent a significant amount of time planning for that game and I always thought we'd get about 5,000," said Foxall. "I never thought we'd sell out the ground but one day we sold 1,500 tickets – in one day! It was astonishing. You couldn't buy a ticket and apparently they were selling them on eBay. There was a whole galvanising of the city and that game wasn't just momentous because we stayed up, I think it sent a big message to everyone about the importance of sport and the big potential here."

Despite the incredible pressure of the situation and the increased attention from the Welsh media and beyond, Flynn attempted to keep the players as relaxed as possible. Along with his assistant Wayne Hatswell and mentor Lennie Lawrence, the caretaker boss wanted to shield the squad from the tension and he came up with a novel approach to keep spirits high.

"Ever since Wayne and I took charge we had tried to put a smile back on the players' faces," explained Flynn. We got everyone in the same room together, all eating together and even the ones who were out of favour or injured, we made them feel involved and I told the boys that if they didn't call me gaffer they'd get a £5 fine.

"People like Darren Jones and Pipey have been calling me Flynny for years so I got a load of fines from them. I'd go round the training ground and try to stitch them up. As soon as they talked to me and called me Flynny it was a £5 fine. The Friday before the Notts County game there was seven or eight of them who owed fines. Some of them were £20, some of them were £40 and it had to be paid up that day.

"I knew a lot of them didn't have the money on them and they were going to try to blag it so I said to them we'd make it double or quits. The chef gave me a pound coin and we tossed the coin. The first player up won and had his fine written off. The players were all running round and cheering while me and Hats were fuming and Lennie was just watching on thinking 'what is going on here?'

"Everyone gathered round and the second one won, the third one they win, and the fourth, the fifth, the sixth. I've never seen anything like it. It was the unluckiest coin you've ever seen. By this point me and Hats were getting quite bitter but the players were all dancing round. We won the seventh one but the eighth one they won again, and the ninth. The next two they won and then we won the last one – so we only won two out of 12. We couldn't believe it.

"The players were going mad, bouncing around the training ground because only two of them had to pay a fine. They'd saved themselves about £200 between them and they were delighted. Lennie turned to me and said 'Michael, I have not seen a training ground like this for 15 or 20 years. This is unbelievable.' And this was the day before one of the biggest games in the club's history! But that's what we wanted. We wanted them to be relaxed. We didn't put any pressure on them or build it up. We had to keep them away from that.

"Me, Hats and Lennie had to take the pressure on our shoulders. Everyone from the chef to James Bittner, the goalkeeping coach, Adam Brown, the physio, and all the board – everybody pulled together. And to get nearly 7,500 at Rodney Parade when we could go out of the Football League shows that we've got something special here."

15

A Hard Day's Night

"If you were making a film this is the script you'd use"
Gavin Foxall

With all the final day fixtures kicking off at 5.30pm on Saturday, May 6, there were a few extra hours for the tension to build.

The pubs surrounding Rodney Parade were flooded by a sea of amber shirts from early afternoon as supporters looked to ease their nerves but that wasn't an option for Newport County caretaker manager Michael Flynn and his players. "The nerves were there but the excitement was there as well," said Flynn. "If you can't get excited for a game of that magnitude then you're in the wrong profession."

Hartlepool United's home clash with Doncaster Rovers, which would have implications at the top as well as the bottom of the League Two table, was selected for live TV coverage by Sky Sports. That meant it was even easier to keep track of events at Victoria Park and the Exiles had a man watching the action in the dugout.

"Danny Elliott, a really good coach with the youth team, was on the bench monitoring the Hartlepool game on his phone," revealed Flynn. "Danny helps Wayne [Hatswell] with the warm-

Christian Malcolm @ @ChristianM200   ‌Follow

Got my fingers, legs, toes and anything else I can cross for @NewportCounty and @flynnster17 today. Good luck lads! Stay strong! #survival

RETWEETS 21   LIKES 74

12:22 PM - 6 May 2017

Chris Gunter @ @Chrisgunter16   Following

All the very best to @NewportCounty today. Really hope you do it.

RETWEETS 59   LIKES 318

4:43 PM - 6 May 2017

There was no shortage of support for The Exiles before the final game

Mickey Demetriou puts the Exiles 1-0 up against Notts County

up because I feel it's best I stay out of the way for that. The players don't want me hanging around and putting nerves into them so I tend to stay in the background. So Danny sat on the bench and he was letting us know how the other game was going. But obviously the crowd were letting us know as well."

The opening half an hour passed without too much incident in Newport or 280 miles north in Hartlepool. Then, just after 6pm, came a crucial 60 seconds in both matches. First, Andy Williams scored to put Doncaster 1-0 up against Pools and, just as that news was making its way around Rodney Parade, County were awarded a penalty.

Striker Lenell John-Lewis, making his first start of the season after missing almost the whole campaign with a serious knee injury, went down in the box under a challenge from Notts defender Haydn Hollis. The assistant flagged and referee Nigel Miller pointed to the spot.

Up stepped defender Mickey Demetriou, voted League Two player of the month for April, to claim a remarkable fourth goal in seven games. The defender showed no sign of any nerves as he coolly slotted the penalty high to the goalkeeper's right to give the Exiles a precious lead.

As the half-time whistles sounded around the country, Flynn's men were five points clear of Hartlepool and looking comfortable. "We were 1-0 up and Hartlepool were 1-0 down and everything was tickety-boo," said co-chairman Gavin Foxall, but football is rarely that simple and the final 45 minutes of the season were to produce perhaps the most dramatic scenes in the 105-year history of Newport County.

After John-Lewis and fellow striker Ryan Bird had both gone close to doubling the Exiles' lead, a momentary lapse in concentration at the other end allowed Notts County to equalise as Jorge Grant took advantage of some ponderous defending to score from close range on 61 minutes.

The noise levels at Rodney Parade dropped dramatically and the mood took another turn for the worse when news came through that substitute Devante Rodney had levelled for Hartlepool against Doncaster. County were still safe but they knew that one more goal for Pools would condemn them to relegation.

In the boardroom the directors were every bit as nervous as the fans. "It was horrible," remembered Foxall. "To illustrate the tension, we had an

Mickey Demetriou jumps for joy in front of the Bisley Stand after netting from the spot

Dubliner Mark O'Brien scores the most important goal of his career

odd moment in the boardroom when one of the directors said Doncaster had scored to go 2-1 up. That went round the room until we looked up at the telly and we could see that they hadn't scored. Someone had sent him a text and it was clearly wrong but it spread. When Hartlepool scored to go 2-1 up the thoughts that were going through my mind are unprintable."

With seven minutes to go at Victoria Park, super sub Rodney slotted in his second of the game to put Hartlepool on course for a first victory since March 14. The news was met with sheer disbelief in the stands in Newport and confusion on the County bench.

"The fans had made it clear what the situation was throughout the match," said Flynn. "But I didn't know Hartlepool had scored their second. It was quite flat at that point anyway because we were drawing. Then James Bittner, who's got a bit of a stammer, suddenly said, 'they've scored'. I said, 'who's ******* scored?' And he was struggling to get the words out but eventually he said 'Doncaster'. So for about two or three seconds I was on top of the world, but then James said, 'sorry, Hartlepool.' You can imagine my response to that – my head was gone for a minute."

Flynn quickly recovered his composure, however, and discussed his options with assistant Wayne Hatswell. "I had to remain calm on the touchline because any nervousness from myself would filter through to the players and jeopardise their performance," he recalled. "As long as I was calm on the touchline and kept a clear head I could influence them, or try to influence them the way I wanted to. I don't know how but I managed to keep hold of my emotions and my feelings throughout the time when we were actually getting relegated. That's why I've got good staff with me."

With Hartlepool winning and County drawing, the teams were level on points but it was the Exiles who were heading for relegation on goal difference. They desperately needed a goal and, for Flynn and Hatswell, desperate times called for desperate measures.

"I think Hats and I both said we needed to throw another one up front and Hats screamed at Mark O'Brien to get forward. Mickey Demetriou was saying 'why not me?' because he'd scored all the goals, but Mark had scored an absolutely world class goal in training the day before and thankfully history repeated itself."

There were barely 90 seconds left on the clock when David Pipe cut back inside his marker on the right flank and sent over a dangerous cross with his left foot. Both Bird and substitute Marlon Jackson jumped for the high ball and both got a touch, knocking it on to O'Brien.

The Irish central defender's only previous goal in nearly 100 games as a professional had been for Southport against Welling United but he showed

An ecstatic Mark O'Brien celebrates his 89th minute winner

The Great Escape was seconds away for a nervous manager

the skills of an international striker as he controlled the ball on his chest eight yards out from goal and, in one swift movement, executed a perfect right-foot volley into the bottom corner of the net.

The goal was met with wild scenes of celebration all around Rodney Parade with even the police and stewards gathered behind the goal jumping into the air. O'Brien's composure disappeared as he ran away in shock and fell to the ground as he was mobbed by teammates.

"He doesn't usually score goals, he stops them," said Flynn. "But it was an absolutely unbelievable finish for a centre-back. He pulled it down off his chest and hit a peach of a volley. If he tries that 10 times in training I'd be surprised if he scores five of them, but that image is everywhere now and he'll go down in the club's history. I was so pleased for him because he's someone who works hard every day. He's got a great attitude and I was delighted for him."

The club directors, all of them long-term fans of the club, could not contain their emotions in the boardroom. "Talking about that moment now I still get shivers down my spine," said Gavin Foxall. "There's meant to be a certain amount of decorum where the directors sit but everybody just went absolutely nuts. It was just a brilliant occasion to be part of."

Tom Owen-Evans and goal hero Mark O'Brien lead the celebrations

Flynn appeared to be the calmest man inside Rodney Parade as the minutes ticked away: "During the last seven minutes, when we were going down, my first thought was for the fans because they didn't deserve that," said the boss. "To be honest, I surprised myself. I could have been feeling sorry for myself but genuinely the only thought going through my mind was 'how are we going get this goal?' And, let's be honest, we didn't look like scoring in that second half.

"It's all about the fans. They all chipped in and managed to buy the club and everything we do is for them now. So that was my only thought for seven minutes. Well, for six minutes because when we went and scored I was just praying for us to hold on."

The final whistle sounded at Hartlepool and County knew that they would be safe, as long as they did not concede again and, after seven agonising minutes of time added on, the Great Escape was finally confirmed shortly before 7.30pm on May 6 as referee Nigel Miller brought proceedings to an end.

Player and fan embrace after the final whistle

"I was massively shocked that Hartlepool had managed to beat Doncaster," said Flynn. "Everybody has a dip in form at some point in the season and Doncaster's happened at the wrong time for us, but we always said that we had to get the win and I'm so glad we did it ourselves rather than Hartlepool losing and us maybe drawing. We did it and that was the important thing.

"I know what it meant to the club, the fans, the city of Newport and I was so glad that we got the job done. There was definitely a feeling of relief and pride. I was so proud to put so many smiles on so many faces. I'm proud of what I managed to achieve in just 12 games as a manager in the Football League. It was meant to be, I think."

Defender Darren Jones, like Flynn born and bred in Newport, was not selected for the final game but he watched from the bench and the veteran centre-back was overwhelmed by what he witnessed: "I was very emotional on that last day of the season because I knew I was leaving and obviously after 89 minutes we were getting relegated," he said. "I was on the bench even though I wasn't a sub and I was stood next to Lenell John-Lewis at the end.

"When the second goal went in the feeling was unbelievable because we knew we were safe then, it was job done, but the whole day was an emotional rollercoaster. It was the best game and the most crazy experience I've had in 16 years as a pro."

16
Escape to Victory

"Nothing compares to this – I will never forget this moment"
Mark O'Brien

There was a funereal atmosphere on Sky Sport's Soccer Saturday show as former England internationals Paul Merson and Matt Le Tissier described Mark O'Brien's goal to presenter and Hartlepool United fan Jeff Stelling.

Those emotions of utter despair were matched at Victoria Park as Pools' 96-year stay in the Football League came to an end, but it was party time at Rodney Parade as Newport County AFC revelled in the completion of the Great Escape.

Despite numerous warnings for fans to stay off the playing surface, police and stewards were powerless to stop the inevitable pitch invasion. Players were lifted onto the shoulders of supporters and manager Michael Flynn also raced from the dugout to congratulate his team.

"I expected to burst into tears after the game but I didn't," he remembered. "I ran onto the pitch and I didn't know where to go. I was running all over the place. I grabbed my boy Edward and my daughter Dionne and my wife

Mission accomplished for Flynn and his team

Ecstasy and agony for Sky Sports presenter and Hartlepool fan Jeff Stelling

Victoria, who started crying but I didn't and I don't know why. I've seen the video back and I've welled up but at the time I didn't cry and I don't know why because I do get emotional. I think it was just the biggest relief I've ever had in football.

"We celebrated staying up but it meant so much more than that, and nd I didn't realise until the Tuesday or the Wednesday afterwards how mentally draining it all was. That's when it hit me."

Goal hero O'Brien admitted he was close to tears after his 89th-minute volley and during the memorable celebrations that followed the final whistle: "Nothing compares to this – I will never forget this moment," said the Dubliner. "It is a highlight of my career – and it will live long in my memory. I'm going to watch that goal over and over again – I will show it to everybody at home. I'm not going to live this down. I can't put into words the feeling when I scored the goal – at one stage I forgot I scored it because everyone was going crazy.

"It's what we've been about the last couple of months – we fight until the end," added O'Brien. "We pushed until the 95th minute and we ultimately got the result we deserved. Words cannot explain it, we had the support of everyone behind us and its more for those fans than anything really."

Asked how he ended up in the penalty area, the central defender said: "I was screaming to the manager and asking if I could go up front. It ended up dropping to me and I just thought I have to blast this as hard as I can and thankfully it went in. When I was on the ground [celebrating] and you

It's no dream, County really did survive

By Andrew Penman
01633 777239
ape@southwalesargus.co.uk
Twitter @argusoncounty

County ..... 2 Notts County 1

A headline that looked improbable a few months earlier

could feel the atmosphere of everyone and knowing what was at stake it was close to taking me to tears.

"You can see how the fans turned out in their numbers and it's as much for the city as it is for us. It means the world to everyone. It's a massive achievement. The final whistle nearly brought me to tears as well. It was just a huge weight off the shoulders, a huge sense of relief."

David Pipe captained the Exiles to promotion via a Wembley play-off in 2013 and his return in January 2017 helped galvanise a squad that was desperately short on confidence. For him, pulling off the Great Escape beats winning promotion to the Football League: "I said that if we stayed up it would be a bigger achievement than the play-off win and I stand by that," said the Caerphilly-born former Wales international. The pressure that was on that [final] game and the turnaround, the points gap, everyone writing us off, add all that together and I honestly think it would be a struggle for anyone to repeat that in that short space of time. The fact we've dug in and done it how we have shows we always believed we could stay up, because if we didn't have that belief there was no way of getting out of there.

"The gaffer is very clever with the people he has brought in, including himself who has galvanised the place like no-one's business. A big mention should go to Wayne Hatswell, who I think is very good for the gaffer, and then you've got someone like Lennie Lawrence, who I can't speak highly enough of. I think it is a collective – the players, the fans, everyone involved.

You walk into shops and everyone's buzzing again. It's a massive collective effort."

Newport was certainly buzzing that Saturday night. After finally making their way off the pitch and completing their media duties the players, coaching staff and directors joined supporters in the city centre to carry on the party.

"It took me a good few days to come down," said co-chairman Gavin Foxall. "We went out in Newport on that Saturday night and I've never known anything like it. We walked into Hogarth's pub and the place erupted. I've never seen anything like it in my life. It was a great evening and the boys deserved it. I can't speak highly enough of the job Flynny, his coaching team and the players did."

The incredible turnaround in south Wales even caught the attention of World Cup winner Thierry Henry, the Arsenal and France legend who'd met County boss Flynn as part of the UEFA Pro Licence coaching course run by the Football Association of Wales in Newport. Henry had sent a good luck message by text when Flynn replaced Graham Westley as Exiles boss in March, and he revealed after the season that he followed County's progress closely.

Congratulation @NewportCounty for your "remuntada" 👍 Who is your "patte gauche"? 😏

→ tfc.info/une-remuntada-…

RETWEETS	LIKES		
42	59		

6:00 PM - 9 May 2017

↩   ♺ 42   ♥ 59

News of the Great Escape travelled fast

"He is the big man," said Henry. "He made the impossible possible. In all fairness, I didn't think that it could be done. We were in contact through a few texts and obviously you send your regards and say 'all the best' but I thought it was going to be a difficult one in the situation they were in – 11 points with 12 games to go - but he made it happen. I don't care if it's League Two, it is a remarkable achievement and he made it happen. It is amazing to make up 11 points with 12 games to go. Amazing."

The emotion of the occasion was written all over Michael Flynn's face

Sky TV pundit Henry added: "It was magical because he had to deal with what he had at the time and find a way to make those guys go on a mission, and they went on a mission with a good general. He analysed the situation well of what was needed at that particular moment and the guys responded. It doesn't matter what the adversities are, you need to adapt in any situation. Whatever challenge there is you have to meet it and he did that by staying up. It's still unbelievable for me and people will remember what he achieved."

Flynn enjoyed the immediate aftermath but he was soon planning for the new campaign after being confirmed as the club's permanent manager three days after the victory over Notts County. "We had a big night out on the Saturday and we had a few drinks on the Sunday," he said. "Me and Hats went to Victoria's mum and dad – Rob and Angela – because it was out of the way. On Monday I was hungover in bed but I had to go in to do some media stuff and speak to the players, and on the Tuesday I was appointed full-time manager.

"Then it all started – all the phone calls from agents, and the press and everyone. That's when the hard work started!"

ST DAVID'S PRESS

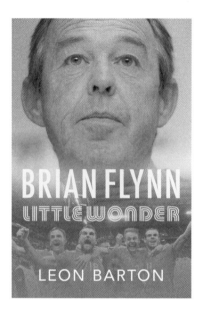

'His name is not only so well-known, but so immediately respected ... everyone should know the story of Brian Flynn.'
Chris Wathan, Chief Football Writer, Media Wales

'One of the good guys of Welsh football.'
Chris Gunter

'A national treasure, Welsh football owes him so much.'
Elis James

'A wonderfully detailed study of the life and times of a Welsh working class hero.'
John Nicholson, Football 365

Little Wonder is the story of Brian Flynn, the stylish yet tenacious midfielder from Port Talbot who, in the 1970s and '80s, enjoyed a successful top flight playing career with Burnley and Leeds United and won 66 caps for Wales. He then achieved success as a manager and coach with Wrexham, Swansea and Wales - where, alongside John Toshack, he recruited and nurtured the Golden Generation that went on to reach the semi-finals of Euro 2016.

Brian Flynn may only stand at 5 foot and 4 inches, but this small man from the town of steel has made a giant contribution to football and *Little Wonder* is his story.

978 1 902719 696 - £13.99 - 224pp - 30+ illustrations/photographs